# Maritime Southeast Asia to 1500

*Sources and Studies in World History*

## Kevin Reilly, Series Editor

# Maritime Southeast Asia to 1500

Lynda Norene Shaffer, 1944-

## M.E. Sharpe
**Armonk, New York**
**London, England**

**Library of Congress Cataloging-in-Publication Data**

Shaffer, Lynda, 1944–
Maritime Southeast Asia to 1500 / Lynda Norene Shaffer.
p.   cm.—(Sources and studies in world history)
Includes bibliographical references and index.
ISBN 1-56324-143-9 (hardcover : alk. paper)
ISBN 1-56324-144-7 (paperback : alk. paper)
1. Asia, Southeastern—History.
I. Title. II. Series.
DS525.S47     1995
959′.01—dc20     95-36663
CIP

Printed in the United States of America

The paper used in this publication meets the minimum requirements of
American National Standard for Information Sciences—
Permanence of Paper for Printed Library Materials,
ANSI Z 39.48-1984.

BM (c)   10   9   8   7   6   5   4   3   2   1
BM (p)   10   9   8   7   6   5   4   3   2   1

Dedicated first of all to Karen Lanette, small consolation
for the tribulations of being the youngest

to Lance Neal, Lonna Nancy, and Lewis Newell III

to our mother, Lola Norene

and to the memory of our father, Lewis Newell II

# CONTENTS

# MAPS AND OTHER ILLUSTRATIONS

**Maps**

**Illustrations**

# FOREWORD

It is with considerable pleasure that I introduce this volume, Lynda Shaffer's second title in the Sources and Studies in World History series. Together with *Native Americans Before 1492* (1992) and a forthcoming book on West Africa, *Maritime Southeast Asia* develops a miniseries of books by Professor Shaffer on important but often neglected regions in world history studies and courses. A projected companion volume will explore some of the structural similarities of these three regions.

Like her earlier study of North America, this work on islands and islandlike communities of Southeast Asia, especially what is today Indonesia, not only shows world historians the importance of the region; it also shows the specialist how an understanding of world history can better define the ebb and flow of regional history. This work vastly improves our understanding of both Southeast Asian history and world history.

Few authors have been able to combine extensive research on the region with global-ranging expertise to such effect. The result is a dazzling array of concise explanations and fascinating meditations on such topics as Malayo-Polynesian migrations, the relation between Central Asian climate and monsoons, land and maritime silk roads, plagues and commerce, Buddhism, "Indianization," and indigenous culture, Turko-Mongolian Islam, and Sufism. These topics, however, are not asides, but provide skeins which, gracefully woven into the tapestry, elucidate Southeast Asian history in ways that purely local knowledge cannot.

In short, this is a history of maritime Southeast Asia for world historians. But it is also a beautifully conceived, lucid, and thoughtful history of island Southeast Asia. With all of its attention to such global matters as crops and language groups, the silk and spice trade, African sailors and Chinese porcelains, scriptural religions and acculturation, merchants and royal houses, this is also a straightforward narrative, rich in traditional political history, which takes us from Funan on the Mekong delta to Sumatran Srivijaya to the kingdoms of Java (ca. 700–1200) to the Muslim realms of Malacca and Mataram, Java, before 1500.

Kevin Reilly

# PREFACE

Several years ago, after disembarking from a plane at Chicago's O'Hare Airport, I was traversing one of the long halls that leads to the hub of the American Airlines terminal. At one point I happened to glance upward and was pleasantly surprised to see a huge globe suspended from the ceiling, a mostly transparent world in which brass-colored land masses were held at the surface, amidst oceans of air. It is a beautiful work of art and for the most part an accurate rendition of the planet, but as I stood staring I realized that something was awry. Indonesia, which now has the fourth largest population in the world, and the Philippines, islands that the United States once treated as its own territory, were missing. Perhaps the artist had decided that shaping and attaching so many islands was too much bother. I, however, was troubled by this essentially American *faux pas.*

Despite the considerable amount of scholarship on Southeast Asia published since the 1960s, courses about the region (with the possible exception of those about the war in Vietnam) are absent from the curriculum of most colleges and universities in the United States. The region is also neglected in most world history courses. Such neglect might suggest that the region has played an insignificant role in major hemisphere-wide or global events, but that was not the case in the past, nor is it true today.

Why much of Southeast Asian history, especially the history of its maritime realm, seems to be missing from the American consciousness is in itself an interesting historical question. With the exception of Thailand, much of the region was colonized, and British, Dutch, and French authorities tended to limit U.S. involvement in their colonies, be it commercial or missionary. The Philippines, is, of course, an exception to this generalization, and our continuing ignorance of these islands, their history, and U.S. relations with their peoples cannot be explained in this way. Even the U.S. involvement in Vietnam and other mainland nations in the decades following World War II does not seem to have spurred any general awareness of the region's culture or history. If Jacqueline Kennedy, fluent in French and influenced by the French awareness of Southeast Asia, had not visited Cambodia's Angkor Wat, one wonders if anyone in the United States, aside from the several hundred scholars who study Southeast Asia, would ever have heard of this world heritage site. It seems doubtful, given that equally important sites are rarely, if ever, mentioned in the world history literature.

It is true that the literature on the early history of Southeast Asia cannot be easily incorporated into world histories. As in most regions of the world, the written sources for the earliest periods are relatively sparse and difficult to interpret. So far, only a limited amount of archaeological work has been done. Conclusions drawn from this work are often controversial, and whenever other sites are dug, there is the possibility that new evidence will call earlier conclusions into question. Such difficulties contribute to the degree of contentiousness that characterizes the scholarly dialogue among those who study the region, and such contentiousness can obscure any consensus that does emerge and tends to discourage those world historians who might otherwise seek to include Southeast Asia in their visions of the pre-1500 world.

The difficulties of interpretation may also have discouraged Southeast Asian specialists from undertaking a comprehensive history of the region. In the third edition of the American Historical Association's *Guide to Historical Literature* (1995), David K. Wyatt, the section editor for Southeast Asia, notes that there has been no major comprehensive view of Southeast Asian history as a whole since D. G. E. Hall's *A History of Southeast Asia,* which was first published in 1955, some forty very significant years ago in terms of the development of historical knowledge about the region. Nor does he recommend without qualification two of the most used studies of the early period, George Coedès's *The Indianized States of Southeast Asia,* the third edition of which appeared in 1964, and Kenneth R. Hall's 1985 *Maritime Trade and State Development in Early Southeast Asia* (Wyatt,

1995: 477, 450–51). The late 1992 publication of volume 1 of *The Cambridge History of Southeast Asia*, edited by Nicholas Tarling, is useful but does not address directly many of the concerns of the world historians, and it presents its own set of problems.

This manuscript was first drafted in 1984, two years after the History Department at Tufts started offering a two-semester team-taught course in world history. The design and development of this course was assisted by a pilot grant from the National Endowment for the Humanities, and the initial drafting of the manuscript was assisted by a Mina Shaughnessy Scholarship from the U.S. Department of Education (FIPSE). Subsequent revisions were facilitated by an appointment as scholar in residence at the Tufts University European Center in Talloires, France, and a Tufts University Summer Faculty Fellowship Award.

Originally the manuscript was intended to provide a historical background for a unit on maritime Southeast Asia in our team-taught world history course, and thus it was structured by the world historical framework within which we worked. Although it has grown in size and scope, its present purpose remains true to its beginnings: to introduce to a world history audience that part of maritime Southeast Asia's history that seems most critical to our concerns. Hopefully it will prompt readers to seek out the specialists' literature on the region and the scholars who produce it. I must add, however, that should readers in this process come across pieces of prose from this publication in an earlier one under the name of one of these specialists, be assured that they first appeared in a version of this manuscript.

Despite obstacles, I have continued working on this manuscript, in its several versions, all these years due to a conviction that a general knowledge of the early history of maritime Southeast Asia should be common knowledge among those who study and teach world history. I am convinced that turning our attention to this region not only will make our vision of world history more complete but will make it more perceptive.

Indeed, Southeast Asia's maritime realm is an excellent vantage point from which to watch the events of world history go by. Since the turn of the first millennium C.E., Southeast Asian sailors have been important actors in world history. Long before the Portuguese arrived in Asian waters, sailors from East Africa to East Asia had already been drawn to Southeast Asian ports. Thus, Southeast Asians and Southeast

Asian history have much to tell us about the shape and dynamics of world history. Indeed, theirs is a unique perspective, revealing some of the less obvious interests of African, Middle Eastern, Indian, and Chinese powers, interests that do not receive much attention in these powers' historical records, nor from scholars who study them in the present. Kenneth R. Hall has begun an examination of these interests in his article "Small Asian Nations in the Shadow of the Large: East Asian History through the Eyes of Southeast Asia" (*Journal of the Economic and Social History of the Orient* 28, part 1 [1983]: 56–88), but much remains to be done.

I would like to take this opportunity to express my indebtedness to William H. McNeill and Alfred Crosby, whose early works sparked my interest in world history and whose more recent work continues to encourage all of us in world history to pursue this endeavor, in spite of the fact that there are easier (although not necessarily more interesting) things to do. They have been most generous with their time and energy, and their advice and support have been indispensable.

I will always be grateful to Michael Weber, the editor at M.E. Sharpe who shepherded this work as well as my earlier one, *Native Americans Before 1492: The Moundbuilding Centers of the Eastern Woodlands,* and Kevin Reilly, the editor of the M.E. Sharpe series Sources and Studies in World History. Their support and encouragement have been constant and indispensable, and without them this book would never have emerged into the light of day. I am deeply indebted professionally, intellectually, and personally to two scholars of Southeast Asian and world history, Lorraine Gesick and Craig Lockard, who have been true friends in uncountable ways. I would like to express my appreciation of all those scholars of Southeast Asia, many of whom I have never met, who have been my teachers through their publications about this important and intriguing place, and to Professor James Roach, my undergraduate teacher at the University of Texas, who first introduced me to this region of the world some thirty years ago, and has remained my friend and advisor through all these years.

I remember with pleasure Phyllis Fischer, who read the first version of this manuscript more than a decade ago and offered excellent editorial advice. A special thanks must go to Sarah Hughes, who read and commented on the manuscript; I hope that she will take a rain check on some of the important suggestions that she made. The illustrations would not have been so numerous and of such quality without the help of Brady Hughes, H. Parker James, and Roger P. Levin. They have all been generous with their aid and expertise. And it is a pleasure to have this opportunity to thank my colleagues at Tufts, especially Li-li Ch'en, Leila Fawaz, Madeleine Fletcher, Howard Malchow, and Patricia Palmieri, for their support and friendship over these many years.

Lynda Norene Shaffer

# 1 INTRODUCTION TO SOUTHEAST ASIA'S MARITIME REALM

**An Asian El Dorado**

In August of 1492, when Columbus set off from Spain on one of history's most momentous journeys, he thought he was on his way to the original Spice Islands, islands within Southeast Asia's maritime realm. Since Europe had no direct link by sea to the Indies (a term that referred to both the Indian subcontinent and Southeast Asia) or to China, he might have tried to repeat the 1487–88 feat of the Portuguese navigator Bartholomeu Dias and sail around the tip of Africa in order to reach the Indian Ocean, but he was convinced that there was a better way. He thought he could find the islands by sailing westward across the unknown ocean that presumably stretched between western Europe and Asia.

When, in October 1492, Columbus had crossed this western ocean and sighted an island realm, he was sure that he had reached his destination, and until the day he died in 1506 he never admitted that the islands and coasts he had encountered on the opposite side of the Atlantic were not Asian. He called these islands the Indies, since that was what he was looking for, and the peoples who already lived in this other hemisphere have been called Indians ever since, a mistake that seems indelible. We now know that he did not find the much desired Spice Islands. Instead, his voyages revealed to Europeans two entirely new continents, lands previously unimagined by them. Ironically, however, Columbus remained frustrated and disappointed because he could not prove that all he had found was a new way to Asia.

Columbus was not interested in discovering a different hemisphere. What he wanted so desperately that he had risked sailing for months into an uncharted ocean was something quite different: to find an all-sea route from Europe to another part of the only hemisphere he knew, to a place that was well known, at least by reputation. He wanted to find the source of the fortune-making spices that were already prized in European markets.

Thus he was seeking islands that had been not only sought but found by long-distance traders for more than fifteen hundred years before Columbus embarked on his fateful journey, islands that in 1492 were already known to mariners all the way from East Africa to Okinawa. The first outsiders to set out in pursuit of the wealth of Southeast Asia's maritime realm were Indians, from the Indian subcontinent, who arrived in the last centuries B.C.E. (Wheatley, 1973: 184). They had come seeking gold and were the first to name a part of the realm "The Land of Gold," a name that later voyagers from the Middle East and China would also give to various locales on the peninsulas and islands of Southeast Asia.

By the first century C.E. this Asian El Dorado had proven to have much more than gold. Indian merchants were also interested in its pepper, eager to augment their own supplies so that they could meet the Roman demand. Although for several centuries thereafter the maritime realm's most important exports would be aromatic woods and resins, gradually the traders of the Eastern Hemisphere discovered the even more profitable rare and "fine spices," cloves, nutmeg, and mace. For more than a millennium before Columbus's voyage, Asian and African sailors had supplied the ports of China, the Middle East, and East Africa with these spices, enriching Southeast Asia's maritime realm as well as their own purses.

Given that so many people for so many centuries were seeking the markets of Southeast Asia's maritime realm, it is surprising that its history before 1500 is not familiar to everyone interested in world history. But most of us in fact know little if anything about the people who created these extraordinarily magnetic spice markets, and thus we remain unaware of those who created the lure that drew so many of the world's sailors out to distant seas, thereby to change the world, and themselves.

## Definitions of the Region

Southeast Asia divides naturally into two parts, the mainland and the islands. Although many similarities, both cultural and geographic, link the two, there are some obvious differences. The mainland possesses long rivers (several flow all the way from the Tibetan highlands) that have formed large plains and deltas, whereas on the islands the rivers are short and fall steeply from mountain heights to ocean shores, a geographical difference that has been associated with certain cultural differences. In general, mainland societies have, for the most part, been preoccupied with their large and fertile plains, while the island peoples have tended to face out across the seas.

Such generalizations always pose problems, and this one is no exception. There are two places on the mainland that essentially belong to the island realm, at least in part because their landforms and topography resemble those of the islands. The southern part of the thousand-mile-long Malay Peninsula is essentially an island, almost separated from the mainland and almost surrounded by sea. Similarly, although less obviously, several hundred miles of the deeply indented and rugged coast of southeastern Vietnam provides a setting more like that of the islands than of the mainland. On the west a thick band of mountains separates this coast from the rest of Vietnam, and on the east thin lines of steep ridges run outward into the sea, creating many long and narrow "island-like enclaves defined by the sea and the mountains" (Taylor, 1992: 153). Thus Southeast Asia's maritime realm, the seaward-looking realm, includes the southern part of the Malay Peninsula and the southeastern coast of Vietnam, as well as the islands.

In addition to the distinctiveness of its geography, Southeast Asia's two parts are clearly marked by a linguistic divide. In the mainland countries of Burma, Thailand, Cambodia, and Laos, and in most of Vietnam, people speak languages that belong to the Mon-Khmer, Thai-Kadai, or Sino-Tibetan families, whereas the peoples of the maritime realm (including the Cham peoples of Vietnam's southeastern coast and the peoples of the southern portion of the Malay Peninsula) all speak closely related Malayo-Polynesian languages. (Singapore, with its large Chinese population, is today an exception to this rule, but prior to the nineteenth century few Chinese lived on its islands, and its people were Malayo-Polynesian speakers.)

This maritime realm is quite large, much larger than most people realize. Defined according to modern boundaries, it includes the countries of Malaysia, Brunei, Indonesia, Singapore, and the Philippines, as well as the southeastern coast of Vietnam. Indeed, were a map of the area superimposed upon one of Eurasia, with the realm's western edge

4

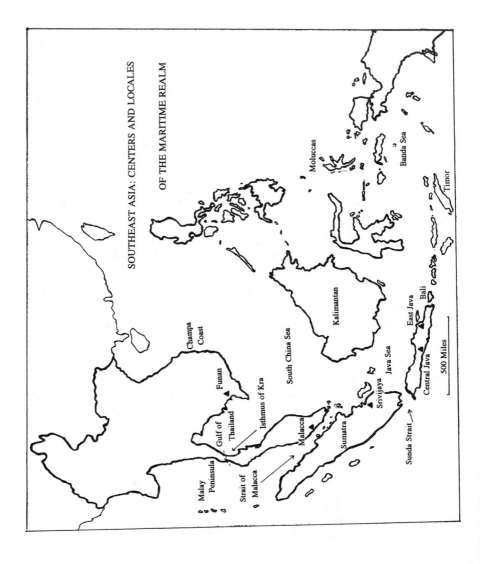

SOUTHEAST ASIA: CENTERS AND LOCALES

OF THE MARITIME REALM

Champa Coast

Funan

Gulf of Thailand

Isthmus of Kra

South China Sea

Kalimantan

Moluccas

Banda Sea

Timor

Malay Peninsula

Strait of Malacca

Malacca

Sumatra

Srivijaya

Java Sea

East Java

Bali

Central Java

Sunda Strait

500 Miles

placed in France, its eastern edge would reach all the way to Afghanistan (see map, p. 6).

Three of these countries—the Philippines, Indonesia, and Singapore—are made up entirely of islands. The Philippines has 7,000 islands that follow a north-south axis for almost 1,000 miles, their land area totaling about 115,830 square miles. (The country's land area is approximately the same as Italy's, although the length of the island group is almost twice that of the Italian peninsula.) Only about one third of these islands have official names, and only about 7 percent are more than a single square mile in area.

Indonesia, the largest country in Southeast Asia, is made up of 13,667 islands, of which about 6,000 have names and about 1,000 have permanent residents. The land surface is approximately 735,000 square miles (an area almost as large as Mexico). From west to east (or east to west) the islands follow the equator for more than 3,000 miles, and if one were to draw a line around them all, the enclosed area (40 percent land and 60 percent water) would be almost 2 million square miles, or more than half the size of the United States (including Alaska).

Singapore, however, with its one main island and fifty-four others, has a total land area of only 238 square miles. Brunei, located on the island of Kalimantan, is ten times that size, with 2,226 square miles. The country of Malaysia includes the southern section of the Malay Peninsula, as well as Sarawak and Sabah, which are again located on the island of Kalimantan, across the South China Sea from the peninsula. Malaysia is thus part peninsula and part island, its total land area standing at approximately 128,300 square miles (which makes it somewhat larger than Norway).

## Malay-Polynesian Origins

A scholarly consensus seems to have formed, although it does not go unquestioned, that the original homeland of the Malayo-Polynesian peoples was not in this maritime realm, with its immense stretches of sea and ocean punctuated by the steep mountain slopes of islands and peninsulas. Before 4000 B.C.E. these people lived in what is now southern China, in coastal areas south of the Yangzi River. This does not mean they were "Chinese" in the modern sense, since southern China at this point in time was culturally quite distinct from northern China. The peoples of the south consequently had relatively little connection

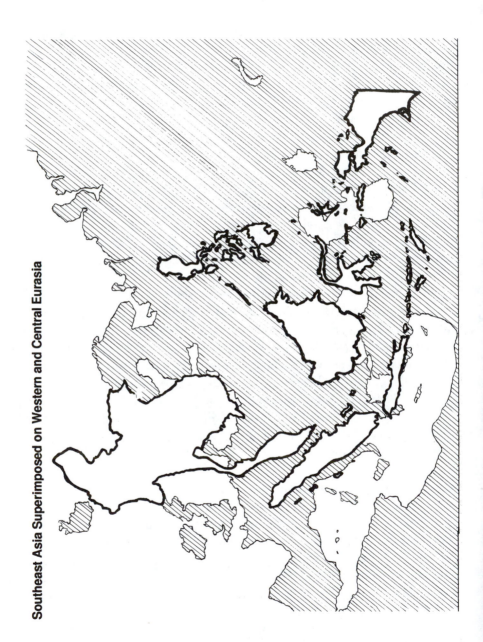

Southeast Asia Superimposed on Western and Central Eurasia

with the ancestors of the Han Chinese who then lived further north, along the Yellow River and its tributaries. In contrast, though, southern China and mainland Southeast Asia were closely related, culturally, ethnically, and linguistically.

Some time around 4000 B.C.E. the ancestors of the Malayo-Polynesians left the mainland, by sea, and settled on the island of Taiwan. From Taiwan they subsequently moved south to the Philippines, and then to eastern Indonesia. Between 3000 and 2000 B.C.E. they went on to settle the islands and peninsulas of Southeast Asia's maritime realm, and those who remained in this realm are now known as the Malays. By 1500 B.C.E. another group, those who would become the Polynesians, had migrated eastward as far as the Bismarck archipelago, northeast of New Guinea. Within a few centuries they could be found in what is now referred to as West Polynesia (Fiji, Tonga, and Samoa), where a distinctly Polynesian culture developed. Polynesian sailors continued eastward, eventually colonizing the most remote islands of Hawaii, Aotearoa (New Zealand), and Rapa Nui (Easter Island) (Finney, 1994: 277).

Rapa Nui, which was settled sometime around 500 C.E., is at least 1,500 miles from any other permanently inhabited island. Its settlers were living some 8,000 miles east of eastern Indonesia, whence their Malayo-Polynesian ancestors had come, and were thus only about 2,300 miles from the coast of South America (Finney, 1994: 284; Taylor, 1976: 38, 42, 52). Indeed, they may well have sailed all the way to South America. Long before any Europeans reached the Pacific Ocean, the Andean sweet potato was grown on some Polynesian islands (including what is now New Zealand) (Finney, 1994: 283), while manioc, another American domesticate, could be found on Easter Island and on other islands in eastern Polynesia. Although some have argued that the presence of American crops on various Pacific islands attests to Native American settlement in eastern Polynesia (Langdon, 1988: 330), the presence of these crops on some of the Polynesian islands could also be interpreted as evidence of contact between Polynesian sailors and South American coastal communities.

## Early Southeast Asia

Long before the first outsiders began to seek out a Southeast Asian El Dorado in the last centuries B.C.E., the peoples of Southeast Asia, both on the mainland and in the maritime realm, were already accomplished farmers, metallurgists, and sailors. The ancestors of the Malayo-Polynesian peoples who lived along China's southern coast were cultivating a domesticated variety of rice by 5000 B.C.E., a full millennium before the maritime migration of the Malayo-Polynesian peoples began. Archaeological sites in Zhejiang, south of the Yangzi River, had revealed that people lived in timber villages, manufactured wooden and bone agricultural tools, wove fibers, made clay pots, had woodworking tools, and kept domesticated dogs, pigs, and chickens. They also had boats, paddles, mats, and rope (Bellwood, 1992: 92), and some of these crops, crafts, and tools could have been carried along by the migrants who became the Malayo-Polynesians. It seems, however, that coconuts and breadfruit were first domesticated in the Philippines and then spread out from there (Bellwood, 1985: 216).

Yet another important cradle of early plant domestication was the highlands of New Guinea, at the eastern edge of Southeast Asia's maritime region. The people who lived here were not Malayo-Polynesian but Papuan. They were one of the original peoples of Southeast Asia's islands, descendants of Ice Age hunters and gatherers who populated many lands off the coast of Asia (including Australia and Tasmania) when glaciers had absorbed so much of the oceans' waters that various land bridges were exposed. When people first came to New Guinea, about fifty thousand years ago, western Indonesia was on the Asian mainland, while New Guinea, Australia, and Tasmania were all part of the same landmass, now referred to by archaeologists as Sahul. Only narrow stretches of water, easily crossed by rafts, separated the mainland from New Guinea and the rest of Sahul (Finney, 1994: 274–76).

Although the dates have not yet been firmly established, Papuan agriculture in New Guinea may have begun as early as 8000 to 7000 B.C.E. (Finney, 1994: 291). Archaeological evidence suggests that many of the crops that became mainstays of the Malayo-Polynesian peoples who farmed within Southeast Asian rain forests were domesticated here. These would include a type of yam *(Dioscorea),* taro (Colocasia, also known as cocoyam), sago palm, and a certain variety of banana *(Australimusa).* The origins of sugarcane are still a matter of discussion. Some authorities associate this crop with southern China, while others believe that evidence indicates it was a domesticate of New Guinea (Bellwood, 1992: 91–94, 113).

## Agricultural Productivity and Demographic Distribution

Because the maritime realm lies on or near the equator, neither the air temperature nor the length of the day varies noticeably as the planet makes its annual rotation around the sun. It does not experience the cold winters of the temperate zone, and except on the highest mountaintops there is no such thing as frost. At sea level the temperature stays near 80° Fahrenheit all year round. Nor do hours of daylight shorten for half the year and lengthen for the other half, as they do in locations closer to the earth's poles.

Even though a frost-free climate is ideal for farming, agricultural productivity in the maritime realm does vary according to soil type. On the mainland farming is most productive on large plains or deltas where long rivers deposit the topsoil of the mountains. In the maritime realm, however, because of its short and steep rivers, only small plains of river-deposited soil exist, and even those are few and far between. As a result, many farmers have to contend with the rain-forest soil of the mountains.

The mountains are indeed covered with tropical rain forests, bountiful providers of fruit, lumber, spice, and aromatic woods and resins. (They were also once home to an abundance of wild life, including tigers and elephants, as well as to bandits, who were often a threat to local law and order.) But rain-forest soil is fragile, and once a field is cleared, it rapidly loses its fertility. This situation gave rise to a form of swidden agriculture, in which the natural vegetation is cleared by cutting it down and burning it off the fields. The fire turns the vegetation to ash, which not only enriches the soil but also kills off any harmful microorganisms and larvae that might be lurking there. A field is then planted and harvested for a few years, until its fertility is exhausted. Thereafter it is abandoned and allowed to return to the forest, while a newly cleared field in another place is farmed. Once the forest has reclaimed the abandoned field, it recovers its fertility and eventually can be cleared and farmed again.

Within the island realm intensive agriculture is possible only in those places where repeated volcanic eruptions have layered the land with fertile and stable volcanic soils. In order to enjoy their bounty, however, people must be willing to live on or near the slopes of volcanoes. On occasion, the same volcanoes that have created the most fertile land can and do erupt, destroying nearby villages and fields and leaving many more buried in volcanic dust. Nevertheless, farmers have been willing to live with the risks. Indeed, the combination of fertile soil, a frost-free climate, and the development of an early-ripening variety of rice well before the third century C.E. made it possible for some to harvest as many as three rice crops a year.

Historically people have tended to concentrate in those places that offer the greatest and most secure food supply, so it is not surprising that those parts of the maritime realm endowed with volcanic soil have also supported the largest and densest populations (Honig and Verdoorn, 1945: 262). This pattern is evident even in contemporary population figures. The island of Java, which has the largest deposits of volcanic soils, also has the largest population in Indonesia. Although its land area is only 7 percent of the country's total, it is home to 65 percent of Indonesia's overall population of 179,100,000. Largely because of Java's population, Indonesia is in fact the most populous country in Southeast Asia, home to 40 percent of the region's total. And after the dissolution of the Soviet Union, Indonesia became the fourth most populous country in the world.

The example of Java underscores a noteworthy fact: it is the productivity of rice that sustains the large populations of monsoon Asia, from Pakistan to Japan. Throughout the region reliable rains and streams have encouraged the planting of rice, one of the world's most bountiful food plants. Until the introduction of Western Hemisphere crops such as corn and potatoes after 1492, no other crop in the Eastern Hemisphere could compete with rice in terms of the amount of food that could be produced on a given plot of land and thus the number of people that could be supported. For example, one crop of rice produces close to 75 percent more calories per acre than a crop of wheat, a mainstay in other parts of the Eastern Hemisphere (Crosby, 1972: 175).

The demographic significance of rice in this part of Asia is obvious when one examines contemporary world population figures. In 1980 the two most populous regions in the world were Southern Asia (which includes both the Indian subcontinent and Southeast Asia), with 28 percent of the total world population, and East Asia, with 26.6 percent. Thus, about 55 percent of the globe's population lives within these rice-growing regions. In short, the remarkably dense populations of South, Southeast, and East Asia are the result of an unusually productive agriculture.

## Metallurgy

Mainland Southeast Asia was also one of the earliest sites of bronze production. Bronze objects uncovered in northeast Thailand were once dated to 3600 B.C.E., but in recent years such early dates have been questioned. Some authorities now say that bronze was first manufactured in the region around 1500 B.C.E., in northern Thailand and Vietnam. Nevertheless, a recent report indicates that there are traces of copper production in central Thailand several centuries prior to 2000 B.C.E. (Bellwood, 1992: 121, 119). Although many more years may pass before the evidence is sorted out, even a date of 1500 B.C.E. for bronze metallurgy is early when compared to the corresponding date for most parts of the world.

Southeast Asian metallurgists took advantage of bamboo, using the hollow segments in the plant's trunk to make a fire-piston capable of producing the high temperatures needed to liquefy ores (Sutaarga, 1971: 9–10). The finest products of this tradition of metalworking are large and exquisitely crafted bronze drums manufactured by people of the Dongsan culture in northern Vietnam from about the fifth to the first century B.C.E. The decorations on the drums, produced by the lost-wax method, portray various economic and political activities, thereby providing an invaluable window into Dongsan culture (Bellwood, 1992: 122–24).

## The Malay Sailors

It is difficult to say precisely when, but by some point in the first millennium B.C.E. the Malay peoples were already intrepid sailors, traveling long distances. Pottery that belongs to the Sa-huynh-Kalanay tradition of Vietnam (dating to ca. 750–200 B.C.E.) has been found in many parts of Southeast Asia, not only in Vietnam but also in Thailand, the Philippines, Malaysia, and Indonesia (Glover, 1979: 178). It was also the Malay sailors who were responsible for the widespread distribution of northern Vietnam's Dongsan drums to various parts of maritime Southeast Asia, beginning sometime around 300 B.C.E. So far, the Philippines and the island of Kalimantan are the only places in the region where these drums have not been found (Bellwood, 1992: 122–24).

The Malay sailors were highly skilled navigators, sailing over the oceans for thousands of miles without a compass or written charts.

**Maritime Southeast Asia (thick lines) Set within the Context of the Southern Seas and Oceans**

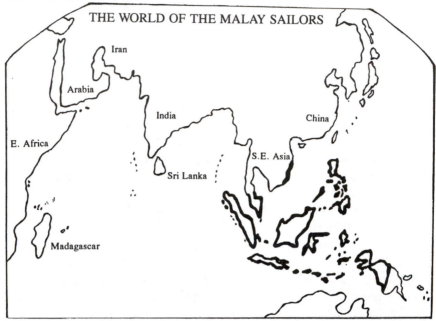

They navigated by the winds and the stars, by the shape and color of the clouds, by the color of the water, and by swell and wave patterns on the ocean's surface. They could locate an island when they were still something like 30 miles from its shores by analyzing the behavior of various birds, the animal and plant life in the water, and the patterns of swells and waves (Taylor, 1976: 30, 45–46). This complex knowledge was passed on orally from generation to generation.

By the third century B.C.E. the Chinese had taken notice of Malay sailors approaching their shores from the "Kunlun" Islands in the southern seas, which the Chinese learned were "volcanic and invariably endowed with marvelous and potent powers" (Taylor, 1976: 32–33). In the Malay worldview, both the mountain heights and the depths of the sea were the site of powerful forces both generous and devastating. The highest reaches of the mountains were holy places, the home of ancestral souls, while the sea contained dangerous spirits that had to be propitiated and then enlisted in one's cause. The Chinese also knew these islanders as builders and as the crews of ocean-going vessels engaged in long-distance overseas trade. The Chinese, in fact, appear to have learned much from these sailors. The Malays independently invented a sail, made from woven mats reinforced with bamboo, at least several hundred years B.C.E., and by the time of the Han dynasty (206 B.C.E. to 221 C.E.) the Chinese were using such sails (Johnstone, 1980: 191–92).

Chinese descriptions of Malay ships, the earliest of which dates to the third century C.E., indicate that the Malay sailed *jong*s (a Malay word), large vessels with multilayered hulls. The English word *junk*, which is often used to refer to Chinese vessels, is a derivative of the Malay *jong*. The Chinese also recognized that their word for Kunlun ships, *buo*, was a foreign word that had been incorporated into Chinese (Manguin, 1980: 266–67, 274). On average, the *jong* could carry four to five hundred metric tons, but at least one was large enough to carry a thousand tons. The planks of the ships were joined by dowels; no metal was used in their construction. On some of the smaller vessels parts might be lashed together with vegetable fibers, but this was not typical of larger ships. The *jong* usually had from two to four masts plus a bowsprit, as well as two rudders mounted on its sides. Outrigger devices, designed to stabilize a vessel, were used on many ships but probably were not characteristic of ships that sailed in rough oceans (Manguin, 1980: 268–74).

The Malays were also the first to use a balance-lug sail, an invention of global significance. Balance-lugs are square sails set fore and aft and tilted down at the end. They can be pivoted sideways, which makes it possible to sail into the oncoming wind at an angle or to tack against the wind—to sail at an angle first one way and then the other, in a zigzag pattern, so as to go in the direction from which the wind is blowing. Because of the way the sides of the sail were tilted, from a distance it looked somewhat triangular (see illustration 1, p. 50). It is thus quite likely that the Malay balance-lug was the inspiration for the triangular lateen sail, which was developed by sailors living on either side of the Malays, the Polynesians to their east and the Arabs to their west.

Precisely when the Polynesians and the Arabs began using the lateen sail remains unknown, but it would seem to have been in the last centuries B.C.E. It is known that the Arabs in the vicinity of the Indian Ocean were accomplished sailors by the first century C.E. and both they and the Polynesians apparently had the lateen sail by then (Hourani, 1951: 102). This pattern suggests that sailors who came into contact with the Malays' balance-lug sail were inspired by it and attempted to copy its design. They might have misunderstood it to be a triangular sail or, in the process of trying to duplicate it, discovered that a triangular sail would serve the same purpose.

Arabs sailing in Mediterranean waters were using a lateen sail by the second century C.E., but it did not appear on Atlantic ships until the fifteenth century, when Portuguese mariners put both the lateen and the traditional Atlantic square sails on their vessels. It was only after they came into possession of the lateen and learned how to tack against the wind that it became possible for them to explore the western coast of Africa, because the winds off Africa's western coast blow the same direction all year round. Without a lateen, Atlantic sailors, including the Portuguese, could not sail south in search of West African gold, since they would have no way to return to Europe. It is ironic that it was an Arabic sail, probably based on a Malay prototype, that made it possible for the Portuguese to round Africa, disrupt the Arab trade routes in the Indian Ocean, and eventually sail into Malay home waters, in pursuit of Southeast Asian spices.

It was also sometime in the first millennium B.C.E. that the Malays made one of the most significant discoveries in the history of navigation —how to ride the monsoons, the seasonal winds of Asia. The cause of this annual wind cycle lies far away in Central Asia, at the center of the Eurasian landmass, as far away from oceans as it is possible to get on this planet and thus a place of extreme temperatures. Because ocean water is warmer than the air in winter and colder than the air in summer, the air close to an ocean is cooled by the water in the summer and warmed by it in the winter. Air masses in Central Asia, however, are so distant from any ocean that they escape such influence, making the winter air in the region much colder in winter and hotter in summer than air over or near the oceans.

It is this difference in temperature between the air mass over Central Asia and the air mass over the far-off oceans that creates the monsoon. During summer the hot air over Central Asia expands and becomes relatively light, whereas the air over the ocean is cooler and thus relatively dense and heavy. As a result, the heavier ocean-influenced air begins to move inward against the lighter air, creating winds that move from the seas and oceans surrounding Asia toward Central Asia. It is almost as if the rising of the hot air over Central Asia creates a vacuum that the ocean-influenced air rushes in to fill. From May to August, when this moisture-laden air mass flows over the continent, it drops a considerable amount of rain on its way inland.

During winter, Central Asia's extreme cold causes its air mass to become dense and heavy, while the air over the ocean is warmer and lighter. This differential in density now causes the heavy Central Asian air to flow out against the lighter ocean-influenced air, so that from December to March dry winds from Central Asia blow out over the continent toward the oceans. During the intervening months the winds are at their most unpredictable. Although in the spring the shift in wind direction occurs rather quickly, in the month of April, the autumn transition from inward to outward is prolonged, causing variable winds from September through November. Taking advantage of this seasonal wind pattern, Malay sailors began to ride the monsoons. They departed with the wind at their back, sailing for thousands of miles to distant locations. There they waited until the winds changed direction, which allowed them to sail home with the wind still at their back.

So far there is little consensus regarding when Malay sailors first reached the East African coast and Madagascar, more than 3,000 miles to their west, but some believe that contact occurred relatively early in the first millennium B.C.E. The uncertain date notwithstanding, in the process of sailing across the thousands of miles of southern ocean, the Malay sailors evidently carried a number of plants from Asia to Africa, including bananas, coconuts, and the cocoyam. (One East African term for cocoyam is derived from a Malay word [Watson, 1983: 68].) The tuning scales of the Malayo-Polynesian xylophone also appear to have ridden with the Malays to Africa, although precisely how this instrument got from East Africa to West Africa, where it can still be heard today, remains controversial (Jones, 1971: 115–19).

The Malay sailors may also have been riding the monsoons of the Indian Ocean to supply the Mediterranean market with cinnamon—a product of southern China—even before the development of an overland or overseas silk route. The Greek word for cinnamon was derived from a Malayo-Polynesian word, through Phoenician and Hebrew. Even though cinnamon was never grown commercially in Africa, Egyptian and Hebrew texts dated to the first millennium B.C.E. speak of cinnamon coming from Africa, leading several scholars to suggest that Malay sailors were responsible for bringing this cinnamon from the coasts of the South China Sea to East Africa. Pliny, writing in the first century C.E., describes an already well-developed trade in cinnamon. The men who brought the cinnamon "put out to sea . . . when the east winds are blowing their hardest; these winds drive them on a straight course . . . from gulf to gulf." Pliny calls their vessels "rafts," a plausible but mistaken description of the Malays' double outrigger canoe (Taylor, 1976: 45). The cinnamon they provided could then have been traded north by the East Africans until it reached Ethiopia, where Mediterranean merchants purchased it.

There is also a thirteenth-century Arab text that refers to a Malay settlement in the vicinity of Aden sometime around the Roman conquest of Egypt in 31 B.C.E. Vast fleets of Malay outrigger canoes came and went from this place, it tells us, but eventually the settlers "grew weak, lost their seafaring skills, and were overrun by neighboring peoples" (Taylor, 1976: 25, 39). According to the text, this happened after Egypt's decline, and scholars have tentatively dated the settlement to the first century C.E.

At roughly the same time Malay communities were established on the island of Madagascar, some 250 miles off the East African coast, where their descendants still constitute the majority of the island's population and Malayo-Polynesian languages are still spoken by almost all. Given the many clusters of islands in the Indian Ocean and the Malay use of islands for navigating, their likely route to East Africa would have been by way of such island clusters, namely, the Maldives, the Chagos, the Seychelles, and the Comores (Taylor, 1976: 30, 45–46).

From linguistic evidence, it would appear that, during these periods of migration, Malay society was made up of many small communities, which they measured by the boatload, even after they were settled on the land. Boat-related imagery persists among peoples living throughout the maritime realm, from the Philippines to Sumatra, the westernmost island of Indonesia (Manguin, 1986: 187, 189), and one scholar has coined the term *oceanic nomadism* to characterize their way of life (Taylor, 1976: 31). What is rather surprising, however, is that even though they spread out over such a large area, the Malay peoples remained closely related ethnically, linguistically, and culturally. In fact, even in the sixteenth century Malay traders spoke a mutually intelligible language all the way from Sumatra to the Philippines (Reid, 1988: 7).

All of these developments—including those in agriculture, metallurgy, and sailing—that distinguished the peoples of Southeast Asia were well underway prior to any significant outside influence on the region. Their roots were well established, and, indeed, some had already blossomed, before any peoples from other parts of Asia began sailing to and through the area. In fact, it is quite likely that Malay sailing and transport of desirable items across the seas, within and without their home waters, played a considerable role in attracting attention to the region and stimulating the first outside interest in its gold. Thus the Malay sailors themselves would seem to have played a leading role in the creation of the maritime realm's reputation as an El Dorado. In subsequent chapters, once international traffic traversed the region, Southeast Asia's story becomes a part of a larger whole, influencing and being influenced by hemisphere-wide developments. At the same time that the peoples of the maritime realm began a momentous cultural dialogue, of their own volition, with trends emanating from the Indian subcontinent, all the better to sustain and nurture their own desires, they were also promoting new products and actively participating in the creation of their reputation as the Spice Islands, a fame that drew sailors from Asia and Africa and ultimately inspired Columbus to undertake the voyage that led to the linkage of the world's two hemispheres.

# 2 IN THE TIME OF FUNAN

## *1st to 6th Centuries* C.E.

Traders from the Indian subcontinent, seeking the source of silk, had begun traveling through Southeast Asian waters on their way to China at least by the first century C.E. The same century also witnessed the emergence of Funan, the first kingdom of size and distinction anywhere in Southeast Asia, at least insofar as the historical record can document. It was located on the mainland, near what is now the Cambodian–Vietnamese border. Sailors from the maritime realm were drawn to its ports, where they could exchange the specialties of the islands for the many and marvelous products available in Funan. By the end of the fourth century, however, the Malays had enticed much of this transit trade south onto a new route that bypassed Funan and carried the traders through the narrow straits now known as Malacca and Sunda. And they had begun to introduce to the world the "fine spices" of the Moluccas—cloves, nutmeg, and mace.

### Maritime Silk Roads and the Emergence of Funan

The earliest silk roads were overland routes that ran from northwest China through Central Asia and Iran to the eastern Mediterranean. These routes had begun developing as early as the second century B.C.E., during China's Han dynasty and the Roman Empire. By the first century C.E. an ever increasing demand for silk had encouraged the development of two maritime silk routes as well, one of which began with an overland journey from western China to India. Large quantities of silk were transported through the Tarim Basin and over the Karakoram Mountains into what is now northern Pakistan and India,

19

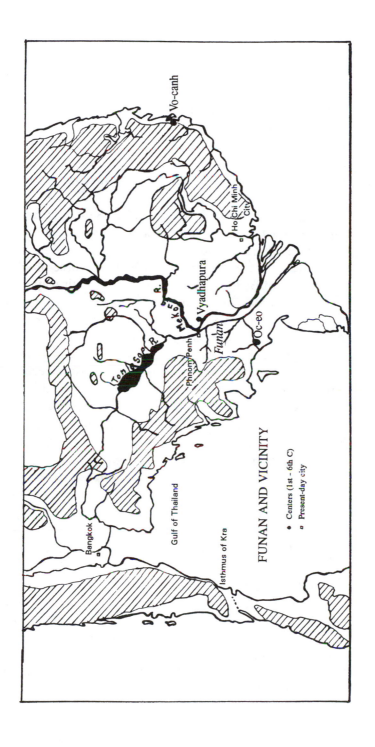

FUNAN AND VICINITY

● Centers (1st – 6th C)
□ Present-day city

Vo-canh

Ho Chi Minh City

Vyadhapura

Funan

Oc-eo

Phnom Penh

Mekong R.

Tonle Sap R.

Bangkok

Gulf of Thailand

Isthmus of Kra

whence the shipments were moved to Arabian Sea ports on India's northwestern coast. Some of this silk was loaded onto vessels embarking for various Persian Gulf ports, but much of it continued on a longer maritime journey that led to the Red Sea, after which the silk was portaged through Egypt, ultimately reaching the Mediterranean (K. Hall, 1979: 38–39). It was also sometime around the first century C.E. that the Yuezhi, a Central Asian people, conquered the entire length of the overland route from China to India, from the Tarim Basin to the Arabian Sea. They established the Kushana kingdom, whose court became an important cultural center.

The other new maritime route passed through Southeast Asian waters, having emerged as a result of merchants on India's eastern coast seeking a direct maritime route to the source of silk in China. Departing from ports near the mouth of the Ganges River, they sailed along the coast of the Bay of Bengal until they reached the Malay Peninsula, which they followed south to its narrowest point, the 35-mile-wide Isthmus of Kra (see maps, pp. 4 and 19). After the passengers and cargo had been transported across this thin strip of land, ships on the other side then carried them along the shores of the Gulf of Thailand until they reached Funan. After spending some time in this locale, they would board other ships for the trip to China.

Although crossing the Malay Peninsula at the Isthmus of Kra required the unloading, overland portaging, and reloading of cargo, most Bay of Bengal sailors apparently had no desire to travel down the peninsula beyond the Kra, and such a journey probably held little appeal for merchants either. Not only would sailing the rest of the way around the Malay Peninsula add an extra 1,600 miles to their trip, but the straits near its southern end are shallow and filled with dangerous shoals and currents. Furthermore, at various times the shores along the straits were believed to be the home of even more dangerous pirates (Fa Xian, 1956: 77).

At first glance it may seem strange that Southeast Asia's first kingdom did not develop on the Malay Peninsula, near the strategic Isthmus of Kra, but on the Gulf of Thailand's opposite shore. The most likely explanation for Funan's success, relative to other potentially competitive harbors on the gulf, was its abundant supply of food. The land around the Kra was covered with rain forest, and its soils would not support intensive cultivation (Peacock, 1979: 200), whereas Funan had the advantage of extraordinary agricultural lands in close proximity to a maritime route. The kingdom was located where an indentation in the coast brought the waters of the gulf closest to the Tonle-Sap and Mekong Rivers, long rivers that had created large deposits of alluvial soil. Their valleys were fertile and wide, and crops could be grown without irrigation owing to the rivers' natural flood patterns. Funan thus enjoyed plentiful and reliable harvests that made it possible to stockpile food both for its own people and for travelers, a capability that may well have been what drew long-distance traders to its ports (K. Hall, 1985a: 48–49, 56).

Providing for travelers journeying back and forth between India and China required large quantities of food. Because of the monsoon patterns, long-distance traders generally could not just stop off in a Southeast Asian port for a few days or weeks. Rather, for half the year, when the winds were blowing off the continent, passengers sailed from India or China to a Southeast Asian port, where they had to remain until the winds shifted and blew toward the continent, at which point they could depart for either India or China. Thus, all the ships, whether they were going to or coming from China, tended to arrive in Southeast Asia at about the same time and to leave at about the same time. The length of time that the travelers might remain in port waiting for the winds to shift varied, but it was generally somewhere between three and five months. Since the port had to feed all the travelers at once, and often for months on end, a Southeast Asian port's access to agricultural surpluses was critical to its success.

There is still much to be learned about Funan. Like many Southeast Asian realms, it has proved an elusive subject. Archaeology has been an important source of information, as have inscriptions carved in stone or impressed on metal. Nevertheless, much of what is known about the kingdom comes from contemporary Chinese accounts, and the very name by which it is now known, "Funan," is in fact the Chinese term for the place, not its Southeast Asian name (which remains uncertain). Nor is there complete agreement regarding the ethnicity of the Funanese. In the past some scholars suggested that they were Malayo-Polynesian, but most now believe that they were linguistically and ethnically Khmer, as the preponderance of the epigraphical evidence would seem to indicate (Jacques, 1979: 374–75).

Funan's core area was located on the Vietnamese side of what is now the Vietnamese–Cambodian border, but there are a number of closely related sites in Cambodia. The capital, Vyadhapura, was established at an inland location, near the Tonle-Sap and Mekong Rivers, during the second century. Vyadhapura can be translated as "City of the Hunter-King," apparently a reference to the second-century king, Hun Panhuang, who went into the forest, captured and domesticated large elephants, trained them for military purposes, and then used them to bring about the submission of his neighbors (K. Hall, 1982: 93). By the early part of the third century the great general Fan Shiman had extended Funan's power westward along the northern rim of the Gulf of Thailand and down the Malay Peninsula as far as the Isthmus of Kra (Wolters, 1967: 37; K. Hall, 1985a: 63–64).

Indian merchants were not the only ones who visited the realm of Funan on their way to China. By the second century C.E. this mainland entrepôt was attracting merchants from the Middle East, and even from as far afield as Greece. Indeed, two men claiming to be envoys of the Roman emperor Marcus Aurelius appeared in China in 166 C.E., having arrived there by way of Funan. It is unlikely that they were truly official envoys: most probably they were Greek merchants (subjects of Rome) who had claimed diplomatic status in order to gain access to the city of Luoyang, which was then the capital of the Han dynasty (Yu, 1967: 159–60, 175; K. Hall, 1985a: 38).

The archaeological remains of at least one of Funan's ports have been found near the present-day Vietnamese town of Oc-eo, which is located somewhat inland, about 3 miles from the coast, as was the settlement connected to the Funan port. Travelers reached it via a network of drainage canals that linked the Gulf of Thailand with the Mekong River (Taylor, 1992: 158). Objects unearthed there include local manufactures, goods exchanged within Southeast Asia, and imports from India, Iran, and the Mediterranean. Ceramics are abundant. Numerous seals and many pieces of jewelry are Indian in origin, and there are tin amulets, apparently made in Funan, with symbols of the Hindu gods Visnu and Siva. Items from China include small Buddhist statues and a bronze mirror, while from the Mediterranean are fragments of glassware, a second-century gold coin, and gold medallions bearing images of Antoninus Pius and Marcus Aurelius (K. Hall, 1985a: 59; Wolters, 1967: 38; Christie, 1979: 284–86).

### Funan and the Malay Sailors

The market that Funan provided attracted Malay sailors from various parts of the maritime realm to its ports. They carried with them supplies and raw materials such as iron for use in Funan itself (Wolters, 1967: 52; 1982: 35n), as well as products that they hoped to exchange for rare goods brought by merchants from faraway lands. Originally the international traders who congregated at Funan, intent on Chinese silk, had little or no interest in Southeast Asian specialties. But the Malays eventually succeeded in introducing their own products into the international trade.

The first such products might be construed as substitutes for the valuable goods that long-distance traders were transporting to China. Among these were frankincense from East Africa and southern Arabia and bdellium myrrh from East Africa, southern Arabia, southwestern Iran, and the dry and rocky areas of India (Wolters, 1967: 105, 113). These substances were usually used to make perfume and incense, but the Chinese used them in medicines as well. During the time of Funan, however, Malay sailors were able to substitute Sumatran pine resins for frankincense and benzoin (also known as benjamin gum) for bdellium myrrh. They also introduced a new product, camphor, a resin that was soon valued as a medicine and as an ingredient in incense and varnish (Wolters, 1967: 65, 103–4, 127). Ever since, the most highly prized camphor has been that of Barus, a port on Sumatra's northwestern coast. Aromatic woods such as gharuwood and sandalwood (a specialty of Timor, about 1,800 miles southeast of Funan) became important trade goods at this time as well (Wolters, 1967: 65–66).

One indication of the significance of Funan to the maritime trade of China is provided by a Chinese mission sent from the kingdom of Wu to Funan in the third century. Wu, which controlled southern China, was one of the regional kingdoms that emerged after the fall of the Han dynasty in 221. Its king, who was interested in foreign trade, had heard that goods from India and other regions to the west could be had in Funan and thus sent two envoys there sometime between 245 and 250. In their subsequent report on this exploratory expedition, they offered the following description of Funan:

> [The people of Funan] live in walled cities, palaces, and houses. . . . They devote themselves to agriculture. They sow one year and harvest for three. Moreover, they like to engrave ornaments and to chisel. Many of their eating utensils are silver. [Customs] taxes are paid in gold, silver, pearls, and perfumes. There are books and depositories of archives and other things. Their characters for writing resemble those of

the Hu [a people of Central Asia who used a script of Indian origin].
(Coedès, 1971: 42; also K. Hall, 1982: 82.)

The envoys' report also assured the Chinese king that this Southeast
Asian kingdom did indeed have contacts with regions further west.

## International Marriages: Lineage and Culture

Since travelers from India resided in Funan for several months at a
time, it is not surprising that Funan's people, especially its rulers,
became acquainted with Indian culture. Although Indian merchants
were probably more numerous, it is likely that the holy men who
tended to follow in their wake, Brahmins and monks, played a more
significant role in cultural dialogues. Local rulers began to adopt and
adapt the most appealing elements of Indian culture, as suited their
own purposes. By the second century Sanskrit names and titles were in
use, and somewhat later appeared inscriptions in Sanskrit and subsequently in local languages written in Sanskrit-derived scripts. By drawing upon Indian culture in this way, these rulers began a regionwide
process often referred to as "Indianization" (Coedès, 1971; Powers,
1993).

References to the "Indianization" of Southeast Asia suggest an im-
plicit comparison with the Romanization of the Mediterranean, the
Sanskritization of the Indian subcontinent, or Sinicization, the spread
of the northern Han culture throughout the Chinese empire and Chinese cultural influence on parts of Korea and the northern part of
Vietnam. However, significant differences exist between the above
processes and what occurred in Southeast Asia, with the result that the
term *Indianization* can be misleading. The rulers of India's Mauryan
Empire (322–185 B.C.E.) conquered much of the Indian subcontinent,
and the emperors of the Han conquered much of what is now China,
plus parts of Korea and Vietnam. The Romans conquered the shores of
the Mediterranean, as well as much of western Europe and England.
Yet none of the Southeast Asian peoples who became engaged with
various aspects of Indian culture was ever conquered or colonized by
Indians.

The relationship of Southeast Asians to Indian culture is thus more
comparable to the Germanic kingdoms' appropriation of elements of
Byzantine and Roman culture (including Christianity) during the Mid-

dle Ages or the Japanese enthusiasm for Buddhism and for Chinese characters and culture during the Nara period and to some extent thereafter. While it is true that Southeast Asian peoples were inspired by many Indian traditions, admiring them and borrowing freely from them, they remained their own masters: foreign material was usually reworked in their hands before being woven into a world of their design. The "Indianization" of Southeast Asia is thus akin to the "Sinicization" of Japan or the "Mediterraneanization" of Germany—terms that historians have never felt a reason to coin.

One authority on the region has suggested that many basic customs and attitudes typically distinguish Southeast Asian cultures from those of India, even in situations where the influence of cultural trends originating in India is obvious. This also seems to be the case with regard to the emergence of kingdoms, despite their decorative overlay of Indian paraphernalia. There is, for example, clear evidence for the persistence of an indigenous sense of hierarchy based on individual powers which might or might not be inherited. For Southeast Asians, it was not so much lineage that mattered as the prowess of the individual and/or of specific powerful ancestors. Nor did it matter so much whether the relevant ancestors were maternal or paternal. Rather, royal descent tended to be cognatic; that is, claims to power could be based either on the mother's or the father's lineage. Essentially, then, the engagement with Indian culture did not alter the basic structures of Southeast Asian societies, and Southeast Asians during this process did not abandon their indigenous value systems or their basic sense of the world (Wolters, 1982: 4–15). Instead, once they became acquainted with the Sanskrit writing system, with Sanskrit political terminology and texts, and with Indian religions, art, and literature, they became creative participants in a larger cultural world.

The Funanese perspective on this cultural dialogue can be discerned from a founding myth that was already old when Chinese envoys recorded it in the 240s C.E. According to one version, the dialogue with Indian tradition began when a female ruler, whom the Chinese called Lin Ye (Willow Leaf), led a raid on a passing ship. One of the passengers, a Brahmin named Kaundinya, led the resistance against her and defeated the raiders. Lin Ye then married the Brahmin, but she did so only after he had drunk of the local waters. The couple subsequently inherited the realm, and seven of its parts were given to their son to rule, while the rest they retained as their own domain (K. Hall, 1985a:

49; Jacques, 1979: 376; D. Hall, 1968: 25–26; Coedès, 1971: 37).

The existence of such a legend does not necessarily mean that a royal marriage actually took place in the manner described. The marriage may well have been metaphorical. But either way, the legend clearly explains that indigenous traditions were fertilized by those of India and that the political integration of larger domains was contemporary with this interaction. It is important to note that a Funanese woman was the initiator of the confrontation, and that it was the foreigner's marriage to her that established for him a place within local society.

Kaundinya's drinking of the water could be interpreted in several different ways. One possible meaning, however, is that he took a water oath, declaring loyalty to the local lineage as an indication that he would serve Funan, just as Indian traditions would eventually serve a variety of ambitious Southeast Asian polities. In any case, the story contains an important moral: good things come not from attacking and plundering passing ships but from befriending them. The story of Lin Ye and Kaundinya thus served to explain the kingdom's rejection of piracy in favor of a mutually beneficial policy of cooperation with travelers.

**Developments in the Maritime Realm**

Although Funan is the best known, it was not the only center flourishing in Southeast Asia during these centuries. Archaeological evidence suggests that political transitions of some variety were underway on Java's northern coast as early as the last three centuries B.C.E. (Wisseman-Christie, 1991: 25). And in the third century C.E., when Chinese envoys were visiting Funan, they heard about a number of other places that lay within the maritime realm. They learned that in "Zhiaying" (most likely on the southeastern coast of Sumatra) there was a king who imported Yuezhi horses from northwestern India, while in "Sitiao" (most likely in Central Java) was a fertile land that possessed cities with streets (Wolters, 1967: 52–61).

These maritime centers appear to have been in the process of appropriating some elements of Indian religion and statecraft, in addition to adapting various indigenous sources of power such as the veneration of illustrious ancestors, in order to enhance their own political positions, or at least to announce their accomplishments and policies. Inscriptions from about 400 C.E. in western Kalimantan and from the mid-fifth century in western Java indicate that at least some had discovered the symbolic power of the Sanskrit script (Kulke, 1991: 4–7). What was until recently thought to be the oldest Sanskrit inscription in Southeast Asia is a rock inscription found at Vo-canh. (The people of Vo-canh, located on the Vietnamese coast near present-day Nha Trang, were Malay-speaking and lived within the coastal area that belonged to the maritime world, in a place later known as Champa.) On the basis of the style of script used, the Vo-canh inscription was once dated to the late second or early third century C.E., but a recent study has argued that it is not much earlier than the fifth century. This study also suggests that Sri-Mara, the king eulogized in the inscription, had no special, subordinate relationship with Funan, as had been proposed in the past. Rather, he should be understood as the ruler of one of the emerging Malay-speaking kingdoms of the maritime realm, similar to those on Kalimantan and Java (Kulke, 1991: 5).

## The Emergence of an All-Sea Route
## through Southeast Asia's Straits

Beginning in the third century C.E. a series of political transformations took place along the various maritime silk routes from China to the Mediterranean, transformations that culminated in the emergence of an all-sea route between India and China that passed through the straits region of Southeast Asia. In the year 226 C.E. a new empire emerged in Iran, bringing with it a resurgence of Iranian power in Central Asia. The Sassanian kings who ruled it were Zoroastrians, and they based their political legitimacy upon a special relationship with the divinity, Ahura Mazda. Then, in 320 the Gupta dynasty proclaimed a new Hindu realm on the Ganges River. Since the expansion of Iranian power had weakened Kushana control over the silk road from China to India, the Gupta kings were able to defeat the Kushanas, unify northern India, and bring much of the subcontinent under their sway.

At about the same time, in Ethiopia King Ezana of Axum transformed his kingdom into a Christian realm. Axum was a long-standing power in the Red Sea region, a kingdom that the Iranian prophet Mani (215–276 C.E.), founder of Manichaeism, had ranked as "one of the four greatest empires of the world" (Kobishanov 1981: 383). It had long been a major trading center, the place where overland trade routes from the African interior (whence came such products as ivory) met up with the maritime routes of the Red Sea and the Indian Ocean. At roughly the same time, moreover, in 330 Constantine I moved the imperial capital from Rome to Constantinople and began the transformation of the pagan Roman Empire into Christian Byzantium.

Initially, the establishment of Sassanian power seems to have caused a slump in trade on the maritime silk route leading from northwestern Indian ports through the Red Sea to the Mediterranean. The Iranians took over portions of the silk roads that the Kushanas had controlled and then apparently diverted much of the silk destined for Indian ports onto overland routes through Iran to the Black Sea and the Mediterranean. This slump did not last long, however, for Red Sea trade was soon revived by an alliance between the newly Christianized powers at Constantinople and Adulis, the capital of the Axumite kingdom in Ethiopia.

Constantine I pursued a comprehensive Red Sea policy, designed to prevent the establishment of any independent power on the Arabian peninsula (Shahid, 1984a: 70), and both he and King Ezana were disturbed by the power of the Sabaeans and the Himyarites, Jewish communities long established in Yemen. During the time that the Sassanians were consolidating their power, these communities had apparently achieved control over much of the trade entering the Red Sea, and the newly Christianized allies even suspected them of being in collusion with Iran. After an Ethiopian invasion of the Yemen in the middle of the fourth century (apparently carried out with Byzantine assistance), the Red Sea trade revived, but with a difference. Unable to do anything about Iran's control over much of the silk trade, the Red Sea ships no longer went primarily to India's northwestern ports. They traveled instead to the pepper ports of southern India and to Sri Lanka.

Many of the ships plying between the Red Sea and southern India and Sri Lanka were Ethiopian. Although the Greeks did have some ships in the Red Sea, they rarely went beyond Socotra, an island off the southern coast of Arabia (Runciman, 1975: 132). However, because the Ethiopian traders used Greek coins to make their purchases, there have been large finds of Byzantine coins in southern India. The dates on these coins testify that this trade flourished from the fourth-century reign of Constantine I until the reign of Justin I (518–527) in the sixth century. Indeed, until the seventh century the Ethiopians remained the predominant commercial power in the Red Sea area (McNeill, 1963: 412).

At approximately the same time that Ethiopia gained control over the Red Sea by invading Yemen, another major development occurred at the opposite end of the great southern ocean. Sometime around 350 C.E. Malay sailors developed the first all-sea route from Sri Lanka to the South China Sea. After boarding a ship at Sri Lanka, passengers sailed straight eastward, through either the Strait of Malacca or the Sunda Strait, to one of the ports on the South China Sea. (A number of such ports seem to have existed in the southernmost portion of the South China Sea, on the islands of Sumatra, Java, and Borneo, which were competing for this traffic—although during the period of Funan's ascendancy, it would appear that none of them managed to gain hegemony over the others.) After a layover, while they waited for the winds to shift, they could proceed to China.

The Malay sailors were thus able to offer international traffic a faster, all-sea route to and from China's silk markets. Travelers departing from India for China no longer had to take ships that clung to the coasts around the Bay of Bengal and the Gulf of Thailand, portaging goods across the Kra in order to reach Funan. By this new route, they could ride swiftly before the monsoons, directly through the straits to ports on the South China Sea. It also meant that cargoes coming from China and maritime Southeast Asia could make a speedier journey to Sri Lankan ports.

## Fa Xian's Account of the New Straits Route

Just how terrifying the new all-sea route could be to first-time travelers is clear from an account written by the Buddhist monk Fa Xian, the first person to describe the route. In 399 C.E., at the age of sixty-five, Fa Xian left his monastery in Changan, China, on a pilgrimage to the home of his faith in northern India. He journeyed to India by an overland route that took him across formidable deserts and over the Karakoram Mountains, through passes at an altitude of 18,000 feet, where the air is thin and any kind of activity, even walking, is difficult.

The most frightening part of his journey had been passing through a deep gorge at the headwaters of the Indus River. He and the other travelers had to pick their way along a narrow path cut into the side of the mountain, which Fa Xian said was "like a stone wall ten thousand feet in height. On nearing the edge, the eye becomes confused; and wishing to advance, the foot finds no resting place." They next had to climb down into the depths of the gorge, descending steep steps again cut into the side of the cliff, and then cross over the river on a bridge made of ropes lashed together (Fa Xian, 1956: 9–10). The travelers had no choice but to inch their way across, even as high winds buffeted the swinging bridge. (The intrepid tourist can now take a bus from China to Pakistan over Fa Xian's route, but all reports indicate that, even with modern transportation, the journey is still only for the strong-hearted.)

Thus in 415 C.E., when the eighty-year-old Fa Xian was planning his trip home to China, he had no desire to return along the same paths over which he had come. Knowing what was behind, but not what was ahead, he gambled, choosing to go home by the all-sea route. What he discovered was that sailing over the oceans could be just as terrifying as trekking over land. He left from Sri Lanka on a merchant vessel carrying two hundred people, but only two days out of port they encountered a gale, which lasted for thirteen days. After the weather cleared, they saw that the boat had been damaged and would soon sink. Just in time it ran aground on an unknown island, where the crew was able to make repairs. However, since they were lost, it took them a while to find their destination. Long overdue and with the rations long gone, they finally sailed into a port on the South China Sea (Giles, 1956: 76–78).

Fa Xian spent almost five months in this port. He does not seem to have enjoyed his stay, his only comment being that heresy and Brahmanism, not Buddhism, flourished there. During the second part of his journey, from this port to China, his boat was once again hit by a storm. After seventy days the crew still had not sighted any land, so they knew they had missed their targeted port—and the entire continent as well. (The normal sailing time to China was fifty days.) So the sailors simply turned left (northwest), because Asia was over there somewhere. When they finally ran aground, they were in Shandong, 1,000 miles north of their destination! They had no idea where they were, but Fa Xian knew he was home when he saw a patch of Chinese vegetables (Giles, 1956: 79).

After Fa Xian's return to China, troubles on the overland silk roads further increased the significance of the maritime route that he had traveled. Northern China had been overrun by nomadic peoples from the Eurasian steppes in the fourth century, which had caused a massive flight of the Chinese population from the north to the south. Since relocation required money and means, it was the more privileged groups who predominated among the refugees, some historians claiming that as many as 60 to 70 percent of the northern upper classes moved south of the Yangzi River. Southern China was not overrun by the invaders, though, in part because horseback riders from the northern steppes could not gallop across rice paddies, and in fact two Buddhist kingdoms, the Liu Song dynasty (420–479) and the Nan Qi (479–502), flourished there in the fifth century.

The immigrants from the north, who had well-established tastes for the products that came from "the western regions," were particularly interested in what they called "Persian" goods. The Sassanian Empire was a major center of trade and manufacturing, and the Chinese believed it to be the source of rare and valuable commodities, many of which, in reality, were neither produced nor traded in Iran. Among the many goods considered Persian at this time were expensive textiles, myrrh, frankincense, alum, cumin, asbestos, amber, pearls, and gems (Wolters, 1967: 129–38).

Until the middle of the fifth century "Persian" goods continued to reach southern China by overland routes that stretched from Iran to China. However, by 428 the Iranians were skirmishing with steppe nomads known as the Hephthalites, or White Huns, who were threatening their eastern frontier. And by 439 the Mongolian Northern Wei dynasty had consolidated its power over much of northern China, including the strategic roads that led west. To make matters worse, the dynasty was being attacked from Central Asia by another steppe people. Given the hostilities all along the overland silk roads, it is not surprising that the flow of so-called Persian goods through northern China to the south was blocked.

Those who had taken refuge in southern China, however, were not deprived for long. Iranian traders increasingly took to the maritime routes, from the Persian Gulf to Sri Lanka, where they could purchase Chinese goods brought to this island entrepôt by Malay sailors (Wolters, 1967, 150–51). Traders from the Persian Gulf region had become firmly established there in the early part of the fifth century (Wolters, 1967: 81), and they arrived at Sri Lanka with many of the desired "Persian" goods. These the Malay sailors could carry back to China, riding the monsoons through the straits.

The Malay sailors who supplied these "Persian" goods sailed to China from ports in Southeast Asia. It is thus not surprising that a southern Chinese demand soon developed for the products of its maritime realm. Not only did the market for resins and aromatic woods remain strong, but China became an inexhaustible market for rhinoceros horn. (In China it was used to make a tonic, guaranteed to overcome male impotence, while in Japan it was used as a charm and hung from the bedposts for the same purpose. As a result of East Asian demand for the horn, the rhinoceros became extinct in Southeast Asia.) The Chinese also became important purchasers of such items as bird feathers, aromatic woods, tortoise shell, and asbestos. And by the late fifth or early sixth century, Chinese consumers were well acquainted with pepper and other Southeast Asian spices. However, because the Chinese tended to think of these spices first and foremost as ingredients in incense or herbal medicines, they referred to this commerce not as the spice trade but as the trade in aromatics and medicines *(xiang-yao).*

## The Moluccan Spices

Among the products that the Malay sailors introduced to international markets were the rare "fine spices"—cloves, nutmeg, and mace— spices that became the most expensive and profitable in the trade. (Cinnamon and pepper were certainly valuable, but unlike these three they were available in considerable quantities in a number of places in southern Asia.) The distribution of large bronze drums, crafted in northern Vietnam, along the coasts of the Java and Banda Seas suggests that Javanese traders may have been acquiring the fine spices in the original "Spice Islands," in the Moluccas (more than 1,000 miles east of Java and 2,000 miles east of the Strait of Malacca), and introducing them into interregional trade networks as early as the second or third century B.C.E. (Wisseman-Christie, 1991: 25). Nevertheless, these spices were not well known in either India or China until the development of the Malays' all-sea route from Sri Lanka to China.

The spice known as cloves is actually the dried, unopened flower bud of the clove tree. Before 1600 the only clove orchards of any commercial significance grew on five minuscule volcanic islands— Ternate, Tidor, Motir, Makian, and Batjan—located immediately off the western coast of the island of Halmahera (Brierley, 1994: 43). Nutmeg and mace were grown in the volcanic soils of the Banda Islands, a group of ten islands in the Banda Sea, directly south of the island known as Ceram (although they are so small, with a total area of

17 square miles, that they do not appear or are not labeled on many maps). What is sold as nutmeg is a kernel found inside the seed, while mace comes from the chewy red rind that covers this kernel.

Given the value that these fine spices acquired throughout the Eastern Hemisphere, it is remarkable that no one managed to break what was tantamount to a Moluccan monopoly until the seventeenth century, when the Dutch seized the spice-producing islands. Throughout the centuries, the islanders had kept a close watch on visitors to prevent the smuggling of seeds or plants. Nor were the Moluccan spice growers, who were highly skilled at tending the trees and harvesting and drying the spices, interested in sharing this knowledge with others. Moreover, even if the smugglers had succeeded in making off with some seeds, it was still unlikely that they would ever harvest a crop. The seeds quickly go bad, and even if successfully planted, the trees often do not grow to maturity. Furthermore, they are exceedingly choosy about where they will grow, being quite particular about soil type, temperature, humidity, the annual pattern of rainfall, and the type of shade provided by other plants. There is a common saying among growers that "nutmegs must be able to smell the sea, and cloves must see it" (Ridley, 1912: 105). Thus, few places in the world could duplicate the conditions on these spice islands.

## The Demise of Funan Amid Sixth-Century Crises

For some five hundred years, until the sixth century C.E., the realm of Funan prospered, long after the development of the all-sea route from Sri Lanka to China. However, around the middle of the sixth century it suffered a precipitous decline, and soon thereafter it was conquered from the north, by the Khmer kingdom of Chenla. Historians have not yet been able to discern the causes of Funan's collapse, but it is worth noting that it occurred almost simultaneously with a series of troubles and transformations all along the maritime trade routes from Constantinople to southern China.

In 520 C.E. the Central Asian Hephthalites broke through the lines secured by the Sassanian military, the shield that had protected both Iran and India. The Sassanian rulers of Iran managed to survive this defeat for more than one hundred years, but Gupta India did not. Owing to external pressures and internal tensions, the power of the Gupta kings eroded, and by the middle of the sixth century their

34

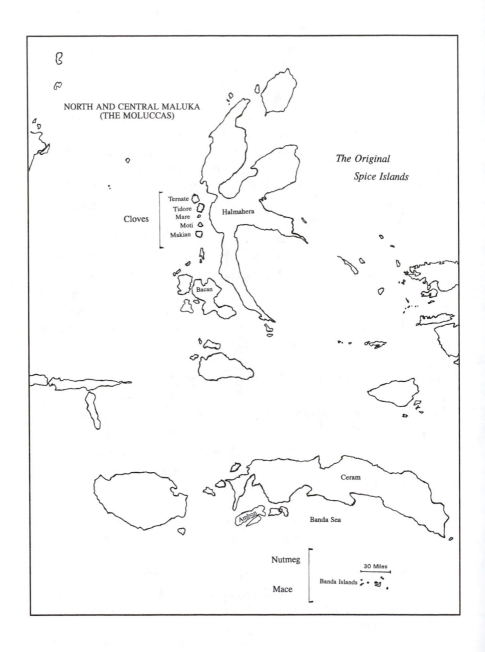

NORTH AND CENTRAL MALUKA
(THE MOLUCCAS)

*The Original*

*Spice Islands*

Cloves

Ternate
Tidore
Mare
Moti
Makian

Halmahera

Bacan

Ceram

Ambon

Banda Sea

Nutmeg

30 Miles

Mace

Banda Islands

empire had fragmented into numerous regional kingdoms. The Red Sea area was also disrupted by hostilities. In the early 520s the Ethiopian king accused the Jewish Himyarites in Najran, north of Yemen, of persecuting Christians, and in 525 he undertook a punitive expedition against them, occupying Yemen for the next forty-five years. From 527 to 532 and again from 540 to 562 Byzantium and Iran were at war. In 570 a Sassanian army crossed the Arabian Peninsula and invaded Yemen, thereby destroying Ethiopian control of the Red Sea. Indeed, the Iranian occupation of Yemen lasted more than sixty years.

Adding to the troubles on the southern maritime trade routes was an outbreak of bubonic plague. In his book *Plagues and Peoples,* William McNeill describes how the epidemic spread from India and other Indian Ocean ports through the Red Sea. By 542 it had hit Constantinople, where an eyewitness estimated that the casualty rate went as high as ten thousand a day (Mango, 1980: 68). Plague and famine continued to devastate the Mediterranean for almost two hundred years thereafter.

McNeill suggests that this outbreak of the plague was a direct result of the close commercial ties between India, Africa, and the Mediterranean. The species of "black rat" that played host to the plague-carrying fleas came originally from India. They were skilled climbers and could easily use the ropes that tied sailing vessels to their moorings to get on and off the ships that moved from port to port. Prior to the sixth-century epidemic the rats had migrated from India to East Africa and the Red Sea, had crossed the narrow land bridge to the Mediterranean, and had spread throughout that sea, although not beyond the Strait of Gibraltar (where Mediterranean ships rarely went until several centuries later). Thus, when the fleas on some of these rats, whether on the Indian or the African coast, became infected with the plague bacillus, the devastating disease was transmitted along the route of "black rat" dispersion (McNeill, 1976: 111–12). Although McNeill does not mention the possibility, it would seem likely that the rats had also dispersed themselves eastward from India, to Funan and possibly to southern China, and that these areas were also hit by bubonic plague at this time.

McNeill further suggests that this outbreak of plague may have been an important cause of the gravitation of power in Europe from the Mediterranean to the north, a process that had begun by the end of the sixth century. At the opposite, eastern end of the southern maritime routes there was also a perceptible movement of power toward the north. Funan was conquered from the north, and in 581 China was reunited when the Sui dynasty (518–618), based in the north, conquered the south.

Across the long middle between these two ends, this northern movement was reinforced after the Muslim conquests of the seventh and eighth centuries. The Umayyad Caliphate, which had its capital in Damascus, gained control over all the routes from China to the Mediterranean, and under their aegis the overland routes prospered, while traffic on the Red Sea route declined. At the same time, the Muslim conquests do not appear to have had a negative impact on the Malay all-sea route through the straits region, for international trade along this route continued to flourish. The Kra portage route, however, never regained its former importance. The age of Funan had come to an end, and from then on, the powerful ports that drew international traders into the region would be located within the Malay world of maritime Southeast Asia, on the islands of Sumatra and Java.

Finally, the sixth century witnessed a momentous economic transformation. Until that time, no one in the Mediterranean region knew the secret of how to produce raw silk; all the silk traded, as well as all the yarn used to make silk, was imported. Thus, in the sixth century, when the hostilities between Byzantium and the Sassanians disrupted the trade routes, a silk crisis resulted. Among other things, silk shrouds for Christian burials were in short supply, Byzantium could no longer appease the peoples on its frontiers with diplomatic gifts of silk, and large numbers of weavers (who used imported yarn or rewove imported textiles) were out of work.

According to Procopius, the problem was solved by one of history's more remarkable acts of industrial espionage. In 551 Nestorian Christian monks told the Emperor Justinian that silk came from cocoons spun by worms that ate mulberry leaves, and by 553, at Justinian's request, the monks had successfully smuggled the worms out of China by hiding them in a bamboo cane, subsequently delivering them to Byzantium (Simkin, 1968: 87). Although experts on the international silk trade now consider Procopius's account apocryphal, they do agree that sericulture, the actual producing of silk threads, was established in the Byzantine lands of the eastern Mediterranean after the time of Justinian (Liu, 1995b: 25). Chinese silk would remain an important item in long-distance trade, but the centuries in which the demand for this product had been the driving force behind new trade routes, both overland and overseas, had come to an end.

# 3 SRIVIJAYA

---

## *Circa 683 to 1025*

### Changes in the Maritime Realm

In 671 the Chinese monk Yi Jing (635–713) set out for maritime Southeast Asia on the first leg of an overseas journey to India. His ship took him to a realm called Srivijaya, a sea power that controlled the straits area between China and India for some 350 years, from the late seventh century to 1025. Unlike Fa Xian, who had decried the absence of Buddhism there some 250 years before, Yi Jing found Buddhism flourishing in the island realm. Indeed, the Srivijayan king patronized monasteries and provided travel money for monks going to India. Yi Jing was so impressed by this Sumantran center's Buddhist scholarship that he even recommended that Chinese monks study there before going on to India.

> Many kings and chieftains in the islands of the Southern Ocean admire and believe [in Buddhism], and their hearts are set on accumulating good actions. In the fortified city of [Srivijaya] Buddhist [monks] number more than 1000 whose minds are bent on learning and good practices. They investigate and study all the subjects that exist in the Middle Kingdom [*Zhong-guo,* the Chinese word for China, here used to refer to the Buddhist heartland in India by its Sanskrit name, *Madhyadesa,* which also translates as Middle Kingdom]. [The] rules and ceremonies are not at all different. If a Chinese [monk] wishes to go to the West [India] in order to hear (discourses) and read (texts), he had better stay here one or two years and practice the proper rules and then proceed to . . . India. (Takakusu, 1896: xxxiv).

Indeed, Yi Jing, a distinguished Sanskrit scholar, spent many years in Srivijaya. Not only did he stay there for six months in 671 while on his journey to India, but he returned in 685, for the most part remaining there from 685 to 695 (Wolters, 1986: 5). Although his concern was exclusively the study and propagation of Buddhism, his writings do reveal, in passing, much of what he learned about the place. The centuries between his own visits and that of his predecessor Fa Xian had witnessed a major political transformation within the region. In Fa Xian's day, there had been many competing ports in the area, but by the late seventh century one of them had prevailed over the numerous contenders to create the realm known as Srivijaya (a Sanskrit name meaning "Great Victory" or "Glorious Conquest"). It exercised hegemony over the coasts in the straits region, on or near the southernmost section of the South China Sea—that is, the coasts of the Malay Peninsula, Sumatra, western Kalimantan, and western Java. Because its dominion spanned both the Strait of Malacca and the Strait of Sunda, Srivijaya was in a position to control the all-sea route between India and China.

One thing that had not changed in the centuries between the two monks' visits was the island realm's literally golden reputation. Foreign travelers were all agreed that this was a rich land, full of gold. Indeed, Arab visitors reported that there was so much gold in Srivijaya that, on a daily basis, the king's subjects ceremoniously threw gold bricks into an estuary. But they were not exactly throwing gold to the waters as one might toss money to the wind. When the king died, the gold would be dredged out, and his successor would then distribute it to the court's allies and retainers, thus cementing their relationship to the new king in a critical moment of transition (K. Hall, 1985a: 80–81).

Chinese writers on occasion referred to Srivijaya as *Jinzhou,* literally, the "District of Gold" or the "Gold Coast," since the term *zhou* usually refers to a coastal area. They also described a hill in Srivijaya (most likely Bukit Seguntang) that was covered with gold and silver images of the Buddha (Wolters, 1986: 21–22, 30; K. Hall, 1985a: 272). During ceremonial feasts the Srivijayans presented golden vessels shaped like lotus flowers to these images as offerings (K. Hall, 1985a: 145). The bowls became well known as a local specialty, and as late as 1082 a Chinese text records that Srivijayan envoys brought golden lotus bowls filled with pearls and other precious objects as gifts for the Song dynasty emperor.

## Palembang as Srivijaya's Center

Although some have expressed doubts about the location of Srivijaya's center, evidence continues to grow that it was on the southeastern coast of Sumatra, in the vicinity of present-day Palembang, a large city located more than 50 miles up the Musi River from the coast. Archaeological studies indicate that what was probably Srivijaya's royal compound was located about 5 miles west of modern Palembang's center in the vicinity of a settlement now known as Karanganyar, between Bukit Seguntang and the Musi River. Bukit Seguntang is a wide hill, with gently sloping sides. Even though it is not particularly tall—its height is only about 100 feet—it is the only noticeable natural landmark near the Musi in the vicinity of Palembang (Wolters, 1979: 5; 1986: 30). Buddhist statues, including the trunk of a large Buddha dating to the late seventh or early eighth century, and old bricks, the remains of a stupa, have been found on its slopes.

South of the hill, in and near the settlement of Karanganyar, houses, irrigated rice fields, tapioca gardens, roads, and small factories cover the ground. Here archaeologists have found the remains of an elaborate complex of canals and tanks that surround an enclosure referred to locally as the "Bamboo Fort." The enclosure, a rectangle that measures about 339 yards long by 252 yards wide (310 by 230 meters), was rimmed by a moat. In the midst of the moat, on the northern side of the enclosure (the side closest to Bukit Seguntang), was an island, where archaeologists have found a considerable number of wafer-shaped bricks that appear to have been part of the foundation of a monumental structure of some sort. Although neither the enclosure nor the canals and tanks have yet been dated, shards of Chinese stoneware and porcelain dating to the Tang (618–906) and early Song (960–1279) dynasties have proven to be plentiful on the surface of both the hill and the enclosure.

Three Old Malay inscriptions have been found in the Palembang area, all of which seem to have been authored by a King Jaynasa (Kulke, 1991: 7). One, dated 682, was found near Karanganyar, and a second, dated 684, northwest of Bukit Seguntang. A third, known as the Sabokingking inscription, undated but from the same general time period, has been found in Palembang's eastern suburbs. In addition, three bronze images of the Buddha were recovered from the Musi River, while Palembang's eastern suburbs have yielded two bronze statues of bodhisattvas (one of which is a large Avalokitesvara) and one bronze Siva. Finally, a garden near the center of the city has yielded an image of Ganesa (the elephant-headed god).

Granted, these remains may be modest in comparison to those found at important sites on the mainland and in some parts of central and eastern Java. Until recently, though, the Palembang area had attracted little attention from archaeologists, in large part because no large stone temple, shrine, or monastery complex still stands there. It may well be, however, that the buildings at Srivijaya's center were constructed of perishable wood and that the walls around its enclosure were essentially a bamboo thicket, which would make their remains rather more difficult to identify. It is most significant that the Palembang area is the only place in the southern part of southeastern Sumatra where considerable amounts of Tang and early Song Chinese stoneware and porcelain have been found (Wolters, 1986: 1–2). Moreover, its location seems quite consistent with Yi Jing's account of local sailing patterns and the natural features between the strait and the city, as well as with those of other Chinese and Arab writers. It would thus seem reasonable to accept Palembang as the original center of Srivijaya, until another locale produces better evidence.

## The International Situation

Muslim merchants had been frequent visitors in Srivijaya's ports ever since the Arab conquests of the eastern Mediterranean, Iraq, and Iran in the seventh century, and in the middle of the eighth century their numbers increased dramatically after the caliphate's capital was moved to Iraq. In 750 the Umayyad Caliphate at Damascus had been overthrown, and by 762 the new Abbasid Caliphate had established a capital at Baghdad on the Tigris River, which flows into the Persian Gulf. There is a tradition that Al-Mansur, the caliph who founded Baghdad, remarked at the time, "This is the Tigris; there is no obstacle between us and China; everything on the sea can come to us" (Simkin, 1968: 81).

The Arab conquest of North Africa, which also began in the seventh century, brought Muslims into contact with cities and towns where trans-Saharan camel caravans arrived carrying gold from West Africa. By 750 significant quantities of gold from the West African empire of Ghana were reaching the lands of the caliphate, thereby increasing its merchants' purchasing power in the rest of Asia and especially in

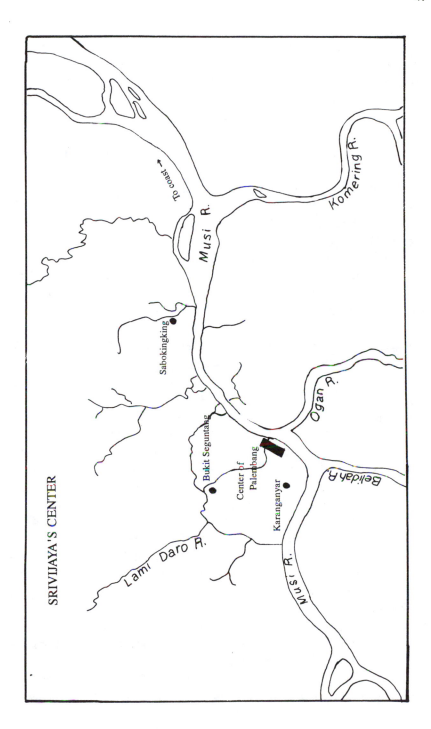

SRIVIJAYA'S CENTER

To coast

Musi R.

Komering R.

Sabokingking

Ogan R.

Bukit Seguntang

Center of Palembang

Karanganyar

Beliдah R.

Lami Daro R.

Musi R.

China, where a large Muslim trading community established itself in the port of Guangzhou (Simkin, 1968: 84). What did lie between the Persian Gulf and China, however, was Srivijaya, the power that controlled the straits of Malacca and Sunda. And the Tang dynasty, in appreciation, granted preferred trading status to ships coming from Srivijaya's ports. Srivijaya also sent tribute missions to China from about 670 to 742 (during the heyday of the Tang dynasty) and from 960 to the eleventh century (during the early Song dynasty) (Wolters, 1979: 14).

Srivajaya's history can also be placed against the background of a Buddhist world that was contracting in its Indian homeland and simultaneously expanding in other parts of Asia. Srivijaya was founded after the fall of India's Gupta Dynasty, which had united much of the subcontinent, as well as after the death of Harsha (r. 612–647), who had succeeded only temporarily in rebuilding an empire in northern India. The regional polities left behind were, like the Guptas, almost all Hindu. Buddhism continued to flourish only under the Pala dynasty that ruled most of what is now Bihar and Bengal, where commercial connections with Southeast Asia remained substantial (Thapar, 1966: 222–23). (The most important Buddhist center in India, the monastery at Nalanda, was located in what is now Bihar.) Meanwhile, the Tang dynasty (618–906) had taken over a reunited Chinese empire, and Buddhism reached the peak of its prestige and importance in China, flourished in Korea, and became firmly rooted in Japan.

It was at this juncture that Srivijaya distinguished itself from its Hindu neighbors by becoming Buddhist. There were many monks who, like Yi Jing, traveled from East Asia to northern India to see the Buddhist homeland and study at the monastic university at Nalanda, the most prestigious in Asia. Since the monks often went by way of the Strait of Malacca, the royal port of Srivijaya became an important center on the pilgrimage route. Furthermore, as Yi Jing had recommended, Chinese monks often remained in the monasteries of Srivijaya for some time, studying in both the Malay and Sanskrit languages, before moving on to India.

Both Hindu and Buddhist literature was written in Sanskrit and in related languages that used its phonetic writing system. By the time of Funan, Sanskrit had become the first written language used by Southeast Asians. Then, during the time of Srivijaya, in the seventh century, Southeast Asians adapted its phonetic symbols in order to write their own vernacular languages and began to translate Indian texts into their own languages. They wrote and painted on *lontar,* palm-leaf slats about the size of a ruler, with holes punched into them so that they could be tied together to form books (Holt, 1967: 88).

## From Local Port to Major Center

Ports along the southeastern coast of Sumatra had begun to gain in importance with the pioneering of the all-sea route around 350 (Bellwood, 1992: 132). At one point in time the port that would become Srivijaya was one of many river-mouth ports in the island realm, small political centers that concentrated the resources of their river's drainage basin near the coast in order to attract traders. They could then use the goods that they secured from the seaborne trade to enhance their own resources, either by holding onto them or by exchanging them with peoples in their upstream hinterlands. Since the shores of the maritime realm were scored through by a large number of relatively short rivers, this dynamic led to the creation of many small polities based at river mouths. These ports tended to look back toward the mountains and forward to the sea, but they did not look kindly to their sides, for neighboring river systems were viewed as rivals and enemies.

The founder of the Srivijayan realm, first mentioned in a stone inscription dated 683 C.E., was a Malay war chief, the ruler of one of the riverine polities. In the latter part of the seventh century, he led a victorious army against Jambi-Malayu, a neighboring river-mouth port located on the Jambi-Batang River. The initial motivation for conquest was probably not so much a desire to control the international trade that passed through the strait as it was a more basic animosity toward Jambi-Malayu. Although both ports were located near the Strait of Malacca, sailors moving down the Malay Peninsula from the north would have arrived first at Jambi-Malayu, since it was closer to the peninsula than the Palembang area, and it appears that Jambi-Malayu had enjoyed an early preeminence.

In order to form this victorious army, Srivijaya's founder had first called together the surrounding war chiefs and their forces, which altogether numbered some twenty thousand. He then selected two thousand from those assembled to form the army that he led against Jambi-Malayu. Most likely the cooperating chiefs came from the Musi River hinterland and were thus willing to place their forces under the command of the port's ruler. After proving himself in battle, the conqueror erected a stone inscription that proclaimed his expectations for his new subjects (K. Hall, 1985a: 83–85).

> The king expressed his concern that all the clearances and gardens made by them should be full [of crops], that the cattle of all species raised by them and the bondsmen they possess should prosper, that all their servants shall be faithful and devoted to them, that, wherever they may find themselves, there be in that place no thieves, no ruffians and no adulterers, that there arise among them the thought of Bodhi [wisdom] and the love of the Three Jewels [the Buddha, the Doctrines, and the monkhood]. (K. Hall, 1985a: 85).

Why it was Srivijaya that won the battles and ultimately captured the international trade through the straits is not immediately apparent. Although its location about halfway between the Strait of Malacca and the Sunda Strait was doubtless significant, a number of other ports, such as Jambi-Malayu, enjoyed equally good locations. Both Srivijaya and Jambi-Malayu had access to the shallow waters of the straits region, one of the world's most abundant fishing grounds (Reid, 1988: 2–3) and a definite asset in terms of providing food for their own population as well as for international travelers. At the same time, neither of them had the advantage of proximity to those places that produced Southeast Asia's trade goods. Camphor came from more northern and western parts of Sumatra, while the important pepper-producing locales were likewise elsewhere on Sumatra or even further afield, on Java. Sandalwood came from Timor, which was about 1,500 miles to Sumatra's east, and cloves, nutmeg, and mace came from the Moluccas, which were equally far away.

One factor in Srivijaya's success may well have been the Musi River. Although none of the river-mouth ports near the Straits of Malacca and Sunda could boast agricultural resources comparable to those of Funan, the Palembang area did have the unusually wide, slow, and silt-rich Musi behind it (Bickmore, 1869: 529). It consequently had a better agricultural base than did its competitors. The river also offered ample supplies of fish, prawn, and bivalves (Wolters, 1986: 29).

A local legend claimed that people first came to live at Palembang only after the waters of the various rivers were weighed and it was determined that those of the Musi were heaviest. In other words, the Musi carried the most silt and could be depended upon repeatedly to deposit this fertile substance on fields adjacent to the river (K. Hall, 1985a: 84). Today some of the best rice land in the area lies right where the archaeological remains are concentrated, in and around the "Bamboo Fort" and Bukit Seguntang, where the Tang and Song ceramic shards are most plentiful (K. Hall, 1985a: 281).

Palembang also offers a fine natural harbor. Even though the city is more than 50 miles inland, the Musi is so easily navigable that even the largest ocean-going steamers of the nineteenth century had no difficulty in reaching its docks (Bickmore, 1869: 533). Indeed, even before the age of steamers, boats could move swiftly upstream from the coast or downstream to it, since the tide would carry them all the way up to the city or back to the coast, depending on whether it was coming in or going out (Wolters, 1986: 31). Palembang is also conveniently located near the confluence of the Musi with three important tributaries—the Komering, Ogan, and Belidah (Wolters, 1986: 2). Moreover, above Palembang both the Musi and its tributaries remain navigable by small boats for many miles (Bickmore, 1869: 533), which would have given the site good access to its Sumatran hinterland and the valuable products of the rain forest.

## The Ways of Power

Even when the rulers of the maritime realm became Hindus or Buddhists, they did not abandon indigenous political traditions. Srivijaya's Buddhist kings still possessed the magical powers of their ancestors, and the creation of the realm was a political feat achieved not simply by force but, as was equally important, by the adroit merging of both local Malay and Buddhist symbols of power and authority, the latter having been imported from India and subsequently adapted. Consistent with the Malay tradition, the Srivijayan kings referred to themselves as "Lord of the Mountain" or "Lord of the Isles" and as propitiators of the "Spirit of the Waters of the Sea." In fact, it was to appease the latter that the king threw gold into the estuary. Furthermore, on a specific day each year the king could not eat grain; if he did, a crop failure might ensue. Nor was he able to leave his realm, for were he to travel abroad the sun's rays might go with him, the skies would darken, and again the crops might fail. And the king's bath water had to be treated with flower petals, since any contact between his person and ordinary river water might cause a flood (K. Hall, 1985a: 85).

The empire that Srivijaya ultimately commanded can be divided into three parts: the core area around Palembang, its Musi River hinterland, and the river-mouth ports that had previously been its rivals. In each of these parts the manner in which Srivijaya ruled was somewhat different. The river-mouth core area was ruled directly by the monarch and his family, the latter serving as royal judges, revenue collectors, or land overseers. The king referred to the cultivators of the royal domain as "my bondsmen," and they constituted the nucleus of the royal army as well (K. Hall, 1985a: 92). There were also central officials who were not of royal lineage, various ministers, clerks, and priests, whose positions were not the result of noble birth but of the skills that they had acquired through a Sanskrit education.

Most likely it was such Sanskrit-trained officials, either Malay or foreign, who facilitated the incorporation of many Indian elements into Srivijayan statecraft. The kings sponsored the production of images of the Buddha and bodhisattvas, with facial features that resembled those of Srivijayan rulers; on these were inscribed traditional curses, which would be visited upon any persons of future generations who deigned to melt them down. This representation of rulers as bodhisattvas made sense within the Malay tradition of erecting stone ancestral seats to venerate dead chiefs, whose spirits afforded a source of sustenance and strength for the living. By putting the faces of deceased rulers on the bodhisattva figures, the Malays identified their illustrious ancestors with these deities, who were also helpmates of the living. There were, for example, many representations of Amoghapusa, the Bodhisattva of Compassion, in the maritime realm. When an ancestor of the ruler was represented as this bodhisattva—the compassionate one who extends his helpful hands to the earth to help those in difficulty—it implied that the current king enjoyed a special relationship with this figure and was thus in a unique position to intercede with Amoghapusa for the benefit of his subjects.

The second part of the empire, the Musi River hinterland, was ruled indirectly through alliances with local elites who were willing to subordinate themselves to the kings at the river-mouth port. This relationship between the port and its hinterland, which in fact predated the rise of Srivijaya, was based on mutual interests. A hinterland's access to seaborne goods, be they material or spiritual, depended upon the strength of its port, while the port depended upon the upriver peoples for manpower (especially to aid in military actions), agricultural resources (to help provision the port), and forest products. Accordingly, a port had to exercise care in consolidating its power over upriver peoples. Their interests could not be neglected or abused for long without cost, since the possibility always loomed that these peoples might move downriver and take over the port.

Although Srivijaya was not reluctant to use military means when necessary, it more often secured hinterland alliances by offering benefits, both material and spiritual, to all who attached themselves to its center and displayed this attachment by their participation in central ceremonies and by answering the call to assemble in times of hostilities. In return for their loyal attendance, the leaders of the upriver populations, most likely through gift exchanges, received some portion of the wealth, in gold and in goods, derived from the seaborne trade. Thus their access to the powerful kings at the port enhanced their position in their upriver locale by enabling them to share in the port's prestige and power.

The king's Buddhist advisors also played a strategic role in the hinterland. The king sent them out from the center to make periodic contact with the local authorities, to encourage the localities to hold religious ceremonies and social pageantry honoring both the king and the Buddhist faith, and to ensure their participation in the royal ceremonies at the center (K. Hall, 1985a: 92–93). As a means of binding the hinterland to the port, the kings also used traditional oaths, backed up by threats of dire consequences to anyone who broke these oaths.

One of the stone inscriptions found in the vicinity of Palembang combined a Malay water oath with a Buddhist image. (See illustration, p. 53.) On the upper rim of the stone was a seven-headed snake, an Indian motif that portrays the cobra as protector of the Lord Buddha. The snake imagery spoke to the Malays as well as the Indians since they, too, had a tradition in which rulers invoked the power of snakes to protect themselves and their realms. Below the snake, an oath of loyalty to the king was carved into the stone, and below the oath was a spout. Apparently water was poured over the snake and the oath and down the spout during the oath-taking ceremony. The oath-takers must have been required to drink the water thereafter, for the text said that if any oath-taker was not sincere, his insides would rot. If he remained loyal, however, he would receive not only a secret formula for the final (Buddhist) liberation of his soul but also the pledge, "You will not be swallowed with your children and wives," the latter a reference either to snakes, which it was believed could swallow humans, or to the possibility of being swallowed up by flood waters (K. Hall, 1985a: 88–89). (The statement in the Funan tradition that Kaundinya drank the waters when Lin Ye married him may be a reference to a similar oath-taking ceremony.)

The subordinated river-mouth ports in the straits area and on the Malay Peninsula made up the third part of Srivijaya's realm (Whitmore, 1977: 143). Although the evidence indicates that Srivijaya never ruled these ports directly, it did expect their representatives to participate in central ceremonials and to facilitate the concentration of the maritime region's products in Srivijayan ports. When it came to dealing with this part of its realm, moreover, it was force, as supplied by a royal navy of Malay sailors, that proved the major expedient.

The Malay sailors who traversed the seas of the maritime realm are often referred to as sea nomads, and in some ways they did indeed resemble the nomadic peoples of the Eurasian steppes. They played a pivotal role in transportation and communications within Southeast Asia and in the creation of linkages among various classical empires such as those in India and China. Also, like the nomads on the steppes, they could be fiercely independent. Strong currents and hidden rocks and shoals made the shallow straits area dangerous, but so did these sailors. If their alliances with the river-mouth ports were not sufficiently rewarding, they could turn to banditry or piracy, preying on the traffic that passed through the region.

An Arab account claims that Srivijayan monarchs had bewitched the crocodiles and had thereby made Southeast Asian waters safe for navigation. The truth of the matter is that using the lure of potential riches, they had enticed the sea nomads into their service. Although Srivijaya's rulers were in no position to exercise direct military control over the sailors, they were able to persuade them to join the port in the harvesting rather than the plundering of maritime trade. The kings apparently struck an agreement to the effect that, in return for a share of the port's revenues, the sailors would no longer engage in piracy, would ensure the safe movement of trading vessels, and would act as law-abiding carriers in the trade. And the kings used their allies to subjugate any rival port that might threaten Srivijaya's hegemony.

This method of manipulating the sea nomads worked, and the royal navy that they provided was crucial to the development of Srivijaya as the major international port and the central treasury for the entire realm. But Srivijaya's dependence on these seafaring nomads meant that it had to attract a steady stream of foreign traders into its ports, for otherwise it would not have sufficient trade goods and revenues to reward the sailors. In such an event, they might strike new alliances with rival ports or revert to piracy.

Even in the overseas portion of the realm, however, force was not the only device employed to deal with potentially rival ports. Oaths and rituals, ceremonial displays of reciprocity and subordination, still found a place, and royal funds were used to endow local institutions and to build monuments in various localities. Thus, Srivijaya's hegemony overseas was marked by monasteries founded and patronized by its kings and by royal inscriptions placed in critical locations. A monastery on the Malay Peninsula, for example, dedicated in the year 775, bears an inscription describing its Srivijayan founder as the "Patron of the Snakes," an obvious appeal to local images of power. Inscriptions containing both local and Buddhist elements can also be found at various strategic points along the Sumatran coast, including one site that overlooks the Sunda Strait between Sumatra and Java (Wolters, 1986: 4; K. Hall, 1985a: 83).

## Srivijaya and the Javanese Sailendras

Srivijaya's success hinged on its location on an international trade route, its fine harbor, its silt-laden and navigable river, and the political and economic talents of its rulers, who subdued the pirates and promoted the region's trade. But there was yet another important element in its success, a close relationship with their coreligionists, the Buddhist Sailendras, a royal lineage located in Central Java, well outside Srivijaya's realm.

Although Srivijaya's agricultural resources were superior to those of any other port in the straits area, it is unlikely that its production was equal to the task of provisioning the ships and feeding international travelers, especially after the dramatic increase in traffic that occurred in the eighth century. Central Java was and is, however, the most productive agricultural region in the island realm. Srivijaya's close relationship with the Sailendras may well have been based on a mutually beneficial exchange relationship that ensured Srivijaya's access to some of Central Java's crops. Thus, any picture of Srivijaya would be incomplete without a consideration of Central Java's temple realm and Srivijaya's relationship to it.

50

1. Bas-relief carving of a sailing craft at Borobudur in Central Java, late eighth century. The ships carved on the Borobudur monument testify to the early development of Malay maritime technology. (Courtesy, H. Parker James.)

2. A Jakarta harbor today. Although most of Indonesia's cargo now moves on modern ships, sailing craft of traditional design are still in use. Dock workers were unloading lumber from the island of Kalimantan when this photo was taken. (Courtesy, Brady Hughes.)

3. A Jakarta harbor today. A close look at the bows of sailing ships still in use reveals some similarities to the ships carved on the walls of Borobudur. (Courtesy, Brady Hughes.)

4. Terraced rice field in Central Java. Volcanic soils make possible the intensive cultivation of rice, which has long supported dense populations on the island. (Courtesy, H. Parker James.)

5. The Sabokingking inscription, also known as the Telagu Batu inscription, late 600s. This carved stone was found at the eastern edge of Palembang, Sumatra, which has been suggested as the locale where the Srivijayan kings assembled their allies. An oath of allegiance was engraved on the stone. Apparently water was poured over the stone and the oath, whence it flowed down the spout before it was drunk by each ally. (Drawing by Roger P. Levin.)

6. Borobudur. Built near the end of the eighth century, Borobudur is one of the world's most impressive monumental structures. A Buddhist pilgrimage that traverses each of its tiers carries one through ten stages on enlightenment. (Courtesy, Brady Hughes.)

7. A corner view of Borobudur's five square tiers. (Courtesy, Brady Hughes.)

8. A vertical view of Borobudur pilgrimage. (Courtesy, Brady Hughes.)

9. A wall panel at Borobudur. (Courtesy, Brady Hughes.)

10. One of hundreds of Buddhas found at Borobudur. (Courtesy, Brady Hughes.)

11. On the three circular tiers at the top of Borobudur, the Buddhas are sheltered by stone latticework in the shape of a stupa. (Courtesy, H. Parker James.)

60

12. Prambanan, ninth century. Prambanan, the largest of the temple complexes built during Central Java's temple boom, was dedicated to the Hindu deities Siva, Visnu, and Brama. It is one of eleven such sites clustered on a plain about ten miles northeast of Yogyakart. (Courtesy, Brady Hughes.)

13. Gunung Kawi (Mount Kawi), Bali. These cave temples, carved from solid rock, are among the oldest monuments on the island of Bali. They are only part of a complex built on both sides of a verdant canyon south of Tampaksiring. They date to the eleventh century, perhaps to a time shortly after the reign of King Airlangga (r. 1016 to 1049). Airlangga was a Balinese prince who became king of East Java through marriage to a woman of East Java's royal lineage. During his reign he extended East Javanese hegemony over Bali. (Courtesy, Brady Hughes.)

62

14. Statue of Visnu. Candi Banon, Central Java, early ninth century. (Drawing by Roger P. Levin.)

Only two hundred some years and less than two hundred miles separate these two quite different representations of Visnu and his manbird mount, Garuda. The earlier statue from Central Java could be compared to various Eurasian traditions, in which power is portrayed by means of a dominant anthropomorphic image. In this work, Garuda almost seems to be an embarrassment and is discreetly tucked behind Visnu's legs. The snakes, if they are snakes, are under his feet where they

15. Statue of Visnu. Candi Belehan, East Java, eleventh century. (Now in Modjokerto's Purbakala Museum.) (Drawing by Roger P. Levin.)

seem to function as no more than a platform. On the other hand, in the later East Javanese work Visnu (said to be a posthumous image of the historical King Airlangga) sits above a larger, more complicated animal world. Garuda, indeed, is larger than Visnu, and the snakes, which are unmistakable, pose with their heads held high. The power of the human is seen within a larger context that has at least an equal claim on the viewer's attention.

16. Candi Sukuh, fifteenth century. Located at the eastern edge of Central Java, 27 miles east of Surakarta (also known as Solo), built during the peak of Majapahit's power. Its unique style has been described as a radical departure in Javanese architecture. Although any actual connection between them is exceedingly unlikely, it often reminds observers of much older temples in Mexico and Guatemala, due to its steep pyramidal design and central staircases leading directly to the top. One might also note the turtles that appear to form the foundation for the temple and for the statuary in front of it. The focus of some of its sculpture upon themes of procreation is also unusual (although not unique) in Indonesia. (Courtesy, Brady Hughes.)

# 4 CENTRAL JAVA

## *Circa 700 to 1025*

During the time of Srivijayan hegemony the most famous rulers of Central Java were the Sailendras, a lineage that from the eighth to the tenth century presided over the most majestic kingdom in Java at that time (Wisseman-Christie, 1991: 26), apparently reaching the peak of their powers from about 760 to 860. In Sanskrit the name Sailendra means "King of the Mountain" (Wheatley, 1983: 239), and these rulers were the first on the island to refer to themselves as *maharajas*, a Sanskrit word meaning "great ruler," thereby implying that the Sailendra ruler was a king of kings (Coedès, 1968: 88; K. Hall, 1985a: 109). This lineage would enjoy extraordinary prestige within Southeast Asia's maritime realm when it was at the height of its power, and long after its preeminence on the island of Java had faded.

The first known ruler of the Sailendra royal lineage was Sanjaya, who is described as "the son of Sanna's sister" in an inscription that has been dated to the year 732 (Coedès, 1971: 87). Sometime after his reign, around the middle of the eighth century, one of his successors converted from Hinduism to Buddhism, and thereafter the rise of the Sailendras was closely linked to "an abrupt rise of Mahayana Buddhism" in Central Java (Coedès, 1971: 89). Relations between the two Buddhist powers, the Sailendras and Srivijaya, were amicable. Although Srivijaya tended to be suspicious of the ports on Java's northwestern coast, from which sailors might contest its control of the straits region, it never exhibited any rivalry toward Central Java. The relationship that developed between the two royal centers appears to have been an alliance of equals and was marked by intermarriage, such marriages joining the Sumatran port of Srivijaya with Java's Kedu

Plain, the home of the Sailendras. This plain, surrounded by rice fields that "clung to the skirts of the volcanoes" (Wisseman-Christie, 1991: 26), was still famous in the nineteenth century as the "garden of Java" (Bickmore, 1869: 49). With its rich soil and its relatively large size, it had become a rice bowl unrivaled in the maritime realm.*

Although Central Java's rulers no doubt benefited both directly and indirectly from the export of their rice, they remained remarkably aloof from matters commercial. The peaks of the Merapi-Perahu Mountains separated them from the ports on Java's north coast. In terms of topography, the rice bowl tilts toward the south, in the direction that its rivers flow. Likewise, its elites would appear to have turned their faces south, with their backs to the mountains, declining to face toward the Java Sea ports, which the mountains hid from their view. Nor, understandably, did they express much interest in nearby southern shores. The waters off the southern coast were dangerous and thus did not attract many traders from afar, on top of which royal centers and pilgrimage sites were all located well inland from these shores (Wisseman-Christie, 1991: 30).

Although foreign merchants bearing sumptuous gifts were sometimes present as honored guests at Sailendra ceremonies, Central Java's rice surpluses reached international ports only through an intricate system of markets. The farmers and artisans of the villages took their produce—principally rice, salt, beans, and dyestuffs—to a periodic farmers' market that came to them on a regular schedule. The merchants who made up this traveling market bought the villagers' produce and conveyed it to wholesalers. Merchants from the ports then purchased the produce from the wholesalers and sold it to merchants who traveled the seas, who delivered it to a port like Srivijaya, where

---

*Francesca Bray's otherwise excellent book, *The Rice Economies: Technology and Development in Asian Societies* (1986), states that rice was introduced to Java "perhaps before the establishment of Majapahit in the thirteenth century" (p. 11). Jacqueline M. Piper, author of *Rice in South-East Asia: Cultures and Landscapes* (1993), says essentially the same thing, citing Bray. Nevertheless, a perusal of the literature on Central Java makes it abundantly clear that irrigated rice was grown there long before the thirteenth century. Jan Wisseman-Christie, one of the leading authorities on the economic and political history of Java, points out that numerous inscriptions testify to its presence in the ninth century. Indeed, she further suggests that, given the extent of its development at that time, it may have been introduced an entire millennium before that date (Wisseman-Christie, 1983: 10–12; 1991: 31.)

the international traffic congregated. Several layers of merchants were thus interposed between Central Java's landed elites and the international traders (Wisseman, 1977: 197–212).

It is therefore not surprising that Srivijaya never tried to subordinate Central Javanese kingdoms. After all, this multilayered marketing system could provide it with the provisions it needed, and besides, none of the Central Javanese kingdoms was interested in becoming an entrepôt for international trade. The layers of the marketing system also acted as a buffer between the land-based elites on the rice plain and seagoing merchants, as well as allowing the rice plain's self-contained and internally focused political arena to remain largely undisturbed by outside interests. A description of the attitude toward international trade of Bali's post-1600 elites, written by the anthropologist Clifford Geertz, would seem to apply equally well to the elites of the Kedu Plain during this period.

> [International trade] was connected to political life eccentrically— through a set of extremely specialized institutions designed at once to contain its dynamic and to capture its returns. The lords were not unmindful of the material advantages to be got from trade; but they were not unmindful either that, in reaching for them, they risked the very foundations of their power. Grasping by habit, they were autarchic by instinct, and the result was a certain baroqueness of economic arrangement. (Geertz, 1980: 87)

## The Temple Boom and Borobudur

The indirect nature of the relationship of its elite to international traders did not inhibit in any way Central Java's inspired incorporation of religious beliefs and cultural trends emanating from India. From the early eighth until the middle of the tenth century, contemporary with Srivijaya's heyday, Central Java witnessed "a veritable construction boom." In a little more than two hundred years dozens of monuments of exquisite design and execution were built on the slopes of the mountains and on the plains of Central Java (Soekmono, 1971: 13), from the area around Magelang to the environs of Jogjakarta. This spate of activity was preceded by the construction of a Hindu temple complex on the Dieng Plateau, about 16 miles northwest of Wonosobo. Dated to the end of the seventh century, it sits in a sediment-filled volcanic crater at an altitude of 6,000 feet (Wheatley, 1983: 238–39). The boom

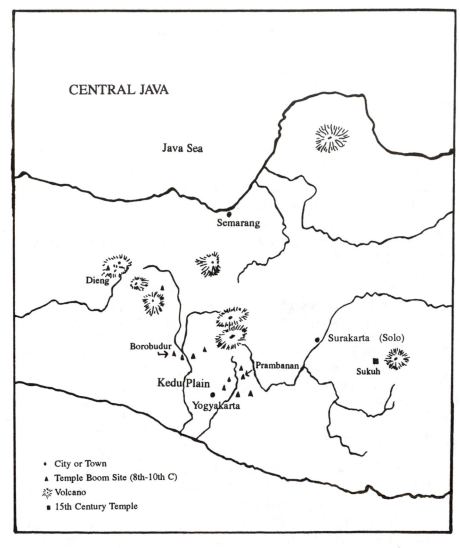

CENTRAL JAVA

Java Sea

Semarang

Dieng

Borobudur

Kedu Plain

Yogyakarta

Prambanan

Surakarta   (Solo)

Sukuh

• City or Town
▲ Temple Boom Site (8th-10th C)
☼ Volcano
■ 15th Century Temple

culminated with another Hindu temple complex at Prambanan, about
10 miles northeast of Jogjakarta.

In between, in both time and space, was the Buddhist monument
called Borobudur, which was built by the Sailendras sometime around
780 and is located on the Kedu Plain, about 26 miles northwest of
Jogjakarta. Like most Central Javanese temples, it was built near a
village on the bank of a river flowing from the Merapi-Perahu ranges,
between 100 and 400 meters above sea level. Pollen samples from the

site indicate that the monument towered amidst agricultural fields and palm groves (Wisseman-Christie, 1991: 27). Indeed, Borobudur must be counted among the wonders of the world. The largest Buddhist monument ever built, and the largest monument of any kind anywhere in the Southern Hemisphere, it is over 100 feet high, while at ground level its square base measures more than 300 feet on each side. The precise meaning of "Borobudur" remains somewhat controversial, but the name can be roughly translated as "Ten Stages in the Accumulation of Virtue" (Holt, 1967: 42; Soekmono, 1976: 41).

The monument's structure is unique, in that it has no interior, nor was it built to shelter worshipers or entomb the dead. Rather, it is a holy mountain, constructed primarily to enlighten the living. Using 2 million cubic feet of volcanic stone, its builders terraced a natural hill, creating ten tiers, which can be divided into four parts. The first part consists of a single tier, originally below ground level. Its walls, carved in high relief, portray a subterranean hell on earth where unenlightened humans are held captive by their greed, lust, and other desires for illusory pleasures. The second part is made up of five square terraces, with 8,235 square meters of carved walls illustrating scenes from the lives of the Buddha and the bodhisattvas. After ascending the square tiers, one reaches the third section, three circular terraces. Suddenly the carved walls have disappeared, and one can see for miles across the plain. Here are found seventy-two three-dimensional Buddhas, each one enshrined under a bell-shaped stupa made of stone latticework. They represent the results of enlightenment, the escape from earthly forms.

Fourth and last is the pinnacle, a single tier covered by a grand stupa, over 15 meters in diameter. Unlike the smaller ones below, the apical stupa contains no Buddha. It is completely empty. Because it does have a large interior space, however, some think it once housed either an image of the Buddha or a relic. At the same time, it would be completely in keeping with the monument's design for its builders to have intended its emptiness, as a fitting image of nirvana, the ultimate extinguishing of material form and the crowning achievement of the Buddhist path. The 3-mile walk up this monument is thus a pilgrim's progress from the depths of human desire, depravity, confusion, and suffering, through the realm of an enlightened but mundane existence, upward to the realm of the Buddhas and ultimately to the complete abstraction and release of nirvana.

The approach to Buddhism displayed by the monument and the episodes from the lives of the Buddha and bodhisattvas carved on its square terraces reflect an international, that is, orthodox Mahayana Buddhism. The style, expert workmanship, and artistic quality of the Buddhas are equal to any found in the Buddhist homeland of India. Nevertheless, there is no question that this is a Javanese monument, built for Javanese purposes. Only the Sailendras fashioned a Buddhist monument in the form of a holy mountain, for in the maritime realm mountains were the locus of powerful progenitors and spiritual forces. They built it with ten tiers, moreover, that scale the monument in the same manner that wet-rice terraces scale the slopes of Java's volcanoes. In fact, this holy mountain may depict more than the Buddhist path of enlightenment: it may also symbolically represent the virtue accumulated by the ten Sailendras who had ruled by the time of its construction (Soekmono, 1976: 40–41).

In the carvings that narrate the lives of the Buddha and the bodhisattvas, the people are portrayed with Javanese features and the scenes are set in Java, not India. (This artistic removal of a religious tradition from one geographic setting to another is not unusual. For example, Flemish and Dutch artists who painted scenes from the Bible peopled them with Europeans and set them in a northern European landscape.) Many of the carvings offer a glimpse of life in Central Java in the eighth and ninth centuries. Among other things are twelve carvings of ships, the best representations available anywhere of the Malay crafts that facilitated the international trade of the southern ocean during these years. The *kala* heads, demon masks carved on the archways over the stairs leading to each new level, are also uniquely Javanese (Holt, 1967: 44). These ferocious images are reminiscent of formidable beasts used in the indigenous tradition to symbolize power and to scare off those who might threaten the sanctity of a site.

## Polities of the Central Javanese Period

This temple boom took place on the volcanic slopes and plains of Central Java, where the political dynamic bore little resemblance to that of Srivijaya and the river-mouth ports of the straits region. One might expect that the centralization of political power would have been readily accomplished on a rice plain, where travel and communication are relatively easy and a political network, like the marketing network knitting it together, would presumably have faced few physical obstacles. Nonetheless, political integration was not as straightforward a task as the plain's geography would suggest, for a great number of local elites, based in what have been called ecoregions, were firmly entrenched.

The power of these local elites was closely related to the demands of farming (van Setten van der Meer, 1979: 97). During the various phases of wet-rice cultivation, the need for water varies widely. When the crop is first planted, the fields must be flooded, but as the plants mature, they are gradually drained, and the ground is allowed to dry out by the time of the harvest. Thus, it was advantageous for all those whose water came from the same stream to coordinate their planting, to stagger it throughout the season so that not everyone was drawing off water at the same time. The need for coordination led to the creation of water boards, organizations made up of representatives from all those villages that depended on the same source of water. The members of these water boards belonged to special lineages, and their participation on the boards reinforced their prestige and power in the villages.

The ecoregions created by the water boards generally corresponded with a network of local shrines, such that those who shared the same water also shared the same local gods. The gods did not permanently inhabit any shrine but rather came down to inhabit them according to an intricate schedule, a schedule that tended to put them in a given shrine at critical times in the planting cycle. Consequently, both the operation of the intricate irrigation systems and the habits of their gods instilled in farmers an acute awareness of the way in which a variety of cycles intersected with one another. The most compelling calendrical cycles that they observed were not those of heavenly bodies but those created by the intersections of human will, rice plant, and river water (Lansing, 1983: 52–53, 57–58).

In the heyday of Central Java, the elite lineages that managed the water boards were always important political actors. As a result, the roots of local power grew deep and held tenaciously, nor were the lineages that controlled these relatively small units eager to give up their local prerogatives. For the members of any one lineage to distinguish themselves and emerge as paramount rulers or kings was not a simple matter, for neither the material resources available to them nor their sources of legitimacy differed substantially from those of their would-be subordinates (K. Hall, 1985a: 115, 269).

When larger kingdoms did begin to form on the Kedu Plain during the eighth century, they were essentially alliance structures in which one ecoregion lineage managed to elevate itself over its neighbors, assert its superiority as a royal lineage, and establish a center with which other lineages found it necessary or beneficial to ally. To do so, they somehow had to acquire a source of legitimacy that would justify their overarching hegemony. It was in this context that Hinduism and Buddhism, and especially the temples and monuments celebrating these faiths, came to play such a prominent role in Central Javanese statecraft, for when rulers who aspired to paramount power introduced such religions, they could claim a relationship to more powerful gods who reigned over universal jurisdictions (K. Hall, 1985a: 115).

These large, impressive, and imposing temples and monuments thus demarcated larger spiritual and political networks that subsumed local shrines and the politics they represented. They also served as centers where a king could demonstrate his spiritual superiority—his connection to these higher gods and to a higher knowledge—through elaborate rituals and state ceremonies conducted by Buddhist or Hindu holy men. And the sculpture that covered the walls of the temples imparted that knowledge to the people. In addition, aspiring kings enjoyed the practical benefits that accrued from the special learning that the holy men possessed. The Sanskrit writing skills of the court-based priests could be put to secular uses such as bookkeeping, which assisted in the administration of the temples and the larger realms the priests served. Furthermore, they provided kings with a royal Sanskrit vocabulary that aided them in magnifying their status relative to that of others (Wisseman-Christie, 1991: 32).

The temples were designed to honor royal lineages, but they were usually built by regional coalitions, with each local constituent contributing a part of the complex. Much of the funding came from gifts that bestowed religious merit upon the donors. Brahmins or monks laid out the temple designs and supervised the work, while royal bondsmen moved the stones and did the rough shaping and chipping. Professional artisans then carved the statues and reliefs. In spite of much theorizing to the contrary, there is no evidence that the construction of such temples placed an undue burden on local populations: in no case did royal demands for labor exceed the king's customary labor rights. If anything, the sculptors' work demonstrates an exuberant creativity, and lighthearted improvisations can be found on many Central Javanese monuments, including those at Borobudur and Prambanan (K. Hall, 1985a: 117–18, 299–300).

The temple complexes grew to be the centers of a politicoreligious redistribution system that operated apart from the ordinary market. Temples usually had rights to a share of local production and local labor, with the result that they became collectors and marketers of agricultural produce and mobilizers of the labor that built religious edifices, as well as bridges, dams, and roads. Like the temples, kings, too, were the recipients of tribute from their allies, tribute that they could exchange for imported goods. These rare and precious items, such as gold, silver, and luxury textiles, were then redistributed with great ceremony by the kings to their allies.

The kingdoms of Central Java were essentially federations. They were constructed of alliance networks, often cemented by marriage, and they were based, at least in part, upon mutually beneficial exchange relationships. Kings did not typically become superior landholders. Nor were their realms bureaucratic or highly centralized states of the sort that would deprive the constituent parts of a separate identity. Rather, theirs was a ritual sovereignty symbolized by the temple complexes and underwritten by the patronage of monks and priests steeped in Indian learning, who endowed a king with sacred powers and reinforced an aura of divine majesty. In short, these kings created ceremonial centers, centers of religion, art, literature, and learning, that attracted their allies and held them in their orbit (K. Hall, 1985a: 118).

## The Sumatran Sailendras and the Demise of Srivijaya

In the middle of the ninth century a civil war wracked the Javanese domain of the Sailendras. The king lost out to an in-law, whereupon he fled to the Srivijayan court on Sumatra. There were then two branches of Sailendras. The Central Javanese branch was still in power on the Kedu Plain in 907, the date of an inscription that lists all the Sailendra kings from Sanjaya to Balitung, then the ruling monarch. The Sumatran branch of the Sailendras seems to have been incorporated into the royal house of Srivijaya. Indeed, as epigraphical evidence indicates, Srivijaya seems subsequently to have used the Sailendra name as its own. When in 860 the Srivijayan king endowed a monk's abode at Nalanda, the monastic university in northern India, the inscription praising the king's benevolence identified him as a Sailendra. In 1005 another Srivijayan monarch provided part of the endowment for a Buddhist temple at Nagapattinam (Suleiman, 1980: 8), the center of the Saivite Hindu Chola realm on India's southeastern coast (Fontein, 1971: 33), and once again the king chose to identify himself as a Sailendra. Both inscriptions were placed in highly visible locations, where not only Srivijayan monks but also Indians and a great many international visitors would see them.

Srivijaya apparently continued to provision its ports with rice from Central Java, even after the civil war of the ninth century and the transfer of power from Central to East Java in the tenth century (Wisseman-Christie, 1983: 10). In fact, it was not until the beginning of the eleventh century that Srivijaya's power faded away. Its hegemony over trade within the maritime realm was first challenged by a new power that had emerged in East Java, and from 990 until 1007 there was periodic war between the two. In 1025 Srivijaya suffered a devastating attack from the Indian kingdom of Chola, and East Java took advantage of the situation by conquering Central Java and severing this rice bowl's ties to Srivijaya. The straits region and Central Java thus lost their preeminence within the maritime realm, and for the next four hundred years the locus of power would shift to East Java.

# 5 EAST JAVA

## *927 to 1222*

During most of those centuries when Srivijaya and Central Java flourished, East Java, including the Brantas River drainage, was a relatively sparsely populated frontier area. Moreover, since its ports were located about 800 miles southeast of the Strait of Malacca, it was, in general, unknown to the international traders who frequented the straits ports controlled by Srivijaya. Yet by the tenth century eastern Java was emerging as one of the most powerful regions in the Malay world and the principal locus of its commerce. From the early eleventh until the early fifteenth century, the most dynamic centers of the maritime realm would all be located in the valleys or on the delta of eastern Java's Brantas River. And along with this eastward shift in the geographical locus of power came changes in economic and political structures, and in aesthetics and worldview.

The kingdoms of eastern Java were the first in the island realm to combine a command of trade equal to that of Srivijaya with agricultural resources comparable to those of Central Java. Its markets became famous throughout the Eastern Hemisphere for their spices and the wealth that the spice trade produced—a wealth so great it was beyond telling, according to the Venetian merchant Marco Polo, who traveled through Southeast Asia at the end of the thirteenth century (K. Hall, 1985a: 210). People from outside the region, including Marco Polo, often assumed that the spices were produced in eastern Java, but that was never the case: the Brantas River region was not an important producer of spices. Rather, the fine spices came from the Moluccas, more than 1,000 miles further east, well away from the straits. Likewise, the pepper in eastern Java's markets was not local but came mostly from western Java and Sumatra. What eastern Java did produce was food—rice, beans, and other staple crops (Wisseman-Christie, 1991: 36). Indeed, it was able to become the preeminent spice market of the Eastern Hemisphere for some four hundred years only because it was in the enviable position of being able to trade its food supplies for the spice growers' stocks.

## International Transitions

The rise of eastern Javanese kingdoms was contemporary with an entire series of transformations that occurred all along the southern maritime routes. In China the Tang dynasty had fallen in 906, and by 960 the Song dynasty had reunited the empire, minus its northern frontiers. Kaifeng, the first capital of the Song, was located in the north, like all previous imperial seats, but it was situated where the Grand Canal crossed the Yellow River, a position that reflected a growing orientation toward the south and the increasing significance of lands south of the Yangzi River, where the canal found its southern terminus among some of China's richest rice lands.

After 1127, when the Song dynasty lost much of northern China to invaders from the steppes, it moved the capital south of the Yangzi River for the first time in Chinese history, to Hangzhou, the city where the canal begins. Not since the days of Funan and the regional Buddhist kingdoms of south China had the Chinese displayed so much interest in the southern oceans. Armed with an amazing array of new technologies—including the compass, printed navigational charts, gunpowder and cannons, and large, ocean-going ships that were true mechanical marvels—the Chinese themselves began to ply the waters between southern China and the spice markets of Java.

Turkic peoples from Central Asia, newly converted to Islam, repeatedly plundered the cities and monasteries of northern India during this period, but a number of new powers flourished on India's southern coasts. One that would have much significance in Southeast Asian history was the Chola kingdom, well known both for its maritime trade and its brigandage. In East Africa, city-states were prospering on the Swahili coast and had begun to engage in shipping and commerce on the Indian Ocean, playing a role somewhat analogous to that of Ethiopia in the era of Funan.

Conditions similar to those prevailing in the age of Funan also were recreated in the Red Sea region during the tenth century. Its trade had been disrupted by plagues and wars in the sixth and seventh centuries, and in the eighth century the Muslim Caliphate had established its capital at Baghdad, near the Persian Gulf, after which the Red Sea route had suffered from benign neglect. However, beginning in the last years of the ninth century, the Persian Gulf area experienced rebellions, civil wars, and invasions, and throughout the lands of the caliphate, local powers successfully challenged Baghdad's control. One of the most successful challengers was the Fatimid Caliphate (909–1171), a Shi'ite power originally based in present-day Tunisia. Between 969 and 973 it conquered Egypt and then brought peace to the Red Sea region. Having revived the Red Sea trade, the Fatimids began supplying both Byzantium and a growing western European market with Asian and African goods, including the spices of the Malay world. It was in fact the rise of the Fatimids that made it possible for Venice to establish its long-lasting relationship with the ports of Egypt (and with other North African ports) and thus its commercial networks throughout western Europe.

It was also after the tenth century, that is, after central Java's temple boom, that powerful kingdoms, the builders of some of the world's most famous monuments, emerged on the plains and deltas of the Southeast Asian mainland. In the eleventh century the monarchs of Pagan sponsored the construction of great temples and promoted the development of Burmese culture, while the temple complex of Angkor Wat was built by Khmer monarchs in Cambodia in the twelfth century. The Ly dynasty (1010–1225) flourished on the plains of the Red River in northern Vietnam, and the Thais were settled on the Chao Phraya Plain, north of the Gulf of Thailand during the centuries that kingdoms in eastern Java were ascendant in the maritime realm.

## The Brantas River Basin

East Java refers, in a political sense, primarily to the drainage basin of the Brantas River. Within the island realm, the Brantas River is unusually long, owing to its circuitous path: it well-nigh encircles a tangle of mountains before finding its way to the sea. Its headwaters gather on the slopes of Mount Arjuna and flow from there in a clockwise direction, first south, then west, then north, all the while gathering the waters of numerous important tributaries. Finally, it makes its way

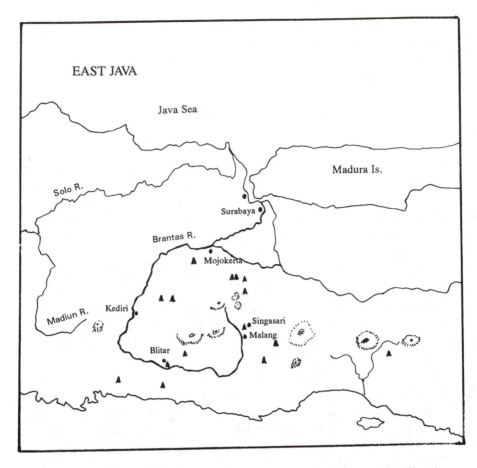

east, crossing a large delta region before reaching the sea. Unlike the rivers that flow through the rice fields of Central Java, then, the Brantas did, in the end, empty out near the northern side of the island, namely, near the all-important trade routes through the Java Sea.

During the time of Central Java's temple boom, the Malay sailors who delivered the fine spices from the Moluccas to the ports of Srivijaya must have passed by eastern Java on their way. However, its ports did not beckon. The Brantas is a turbulent river, and its lower reaches were subject to destructive floods (K. Hall, 1985a: 130). During the centuries of Srivijayan hegemony, the Brantas river delta for the most part remained an area of untilled swamps (D. Hall, 1968: 67). Although there was, by this time, an important center in the Brantas River drainage, it was not near the coast. East Java's earliest known royal city, Kanjuruha, was located in the Malang valley (near Singa-sari), along the upper reaches of the Brantas River, on a fertile moun-tain plateau surrounded by active volcanoes (Wisseman-Christie, 1991: 28; Kulke, 1986: 9–10; also K. Hall, 1985a: 120–21, 302). Kanjuruha is first mentioned in the Dinaya inscription of 760, written in Sanskrit, which reports King Gajayana's consecration of a temple and a stone image of a sanctified Hindu sage. It reveals as well that Kanjuruha's inhabitants included, among others, the royal lineage, principal minis-ters, "groups of leaders," and Brahmins (Kulke, 1991: 13–14).

The accession of King Sindok (r. 924–947) marks the definitive transfer of power from Central to East Java (Coedès, 1968: 128), and by that time foreign traders were present in Brantas River valley ports. One of the inscriptions associated with Sindok, found at Palebuhan and dated to the late 920s, bears witness to a river-mouth port called Goreng Gareng (not yet located) where the king was intent on develop-ing a port under royal patronage and enticing farmers into his realm. There were already many vessels crowding the port, and Sindok was sending both Javanese port merchants and foreign merchants from Sri Lanka, southern India, and Burma into the countryside to collect his taxes (Wisseman, 1977: 207; Kulke, 1986: 9; 1991: 14–17).

Scholars have suggested two important reasons for the transfer of power from Central to East Java around the beginning of the tenth century. On the one hand, Central Java appears to have experienced volcanic eruptions that would have caused considerable destruction, burying many agricultural areas in ash (Wisseman-Christie, 1991: 26–27). East Java, on the other hand, with ports near the Java Sea, seems to have benefited from the growth in international trade. Between 900 and 1060 at least thirty royal charters were issued to trading enclaves in and around the Brantas delta region (Wisseman-Christie, 1991: 39). Early in Sindok's reign, moreover, a Malayu-based force from Srivijaya at-tacked East Java, unsuccessfully. Apparently, then, Srivijaya had by this time recognized in East Java a rival capable of stealing away the spice trade, and hostilities between the two continued for a century (K. Hall, 1985a: 113, 121, 128–29).

## Airlangga

The most famous of East Java's early kings is Airlangga (ca. 991–1049), who ruled for over thirty years, from 1016 to 1049. His capital was at a place called Kahuripan, and since most of the inscriptions concerning him are found in the delta region of the Brantas and Solo Rivers and their environs, historians are confident that the core of his kingdom was relatively near the coast (Kulke, 1986: 9), perhaps not far from Majakerta, on the Brantas River about 40 or 50 miles inland from Surabaya. (Surabaya is today a major city, second in size only to Indonesia's capital, Djakarta.)

Throughout Airlangga's youth (between 990 and 1007) there was periodic war between East Java and Srivijaya. As we saw in the preceding chapter, the end to these hostilities came only in 1025 when the Cholas, rulers of a Hindu kingdom on India's southeastern coast, attacked and plundered Srivijaya. Seizing this opportunity, Airlangga embarked on a program of expansion that would make East Java the new center of the maritime realm. Given that inscriptions bearing his name were concentrated mainly in the Brantas delta region, it would appear that Airlangga's forces did not occupy or rule the lands of subordinated rivals directly (Kulke, 1986: 9). Instead, he essentially extended an umbrella of hegemony over them, such that they would not challenge his supremacy, but otherwise they were left to their own devices.

After he had consolidated his hold over East Java, Airlangga's first acquisition was the island of Bali, which he laid claim to in 1025. His relationship with Bali, located less than 2 miles off Java's east coast, was already close. Airlangga's father was a Balinese prince who had moved to East Java after marrying a woman from its royal family. (Matrilocality was not unusual in the maritime realm, and, as we have noted, royal succession could be either patrilineal or matrilineal.) Bali's economic value lay chiefly in its good volcanic soil and the bountiful rice harvests to be had from the terraced slopes of its mountains. Then, with Bali under his sway, Airlangga went on to subordinate Central Java, the great rice bowl that had supplied Srivijaya's port.

## Damming the River

Another factor in Airlangga's greatness was his successful damming of the Brantas River. Although the delta region was blessed with rich volcanic soil, both its population and its prosperity were threatened by frequent floods. An inscription dated 1037 reveals that the river had burst its dikes in 1033, flooding villages and impeding the progress of ships up the river to the royal port at Hujung Galah. (Its exact site has not yet been discovered, but it is presumed to be in the vicinity of Majakerta.) The local people suffered great losses, and the king was concerned about the damage to commercial revenues. Airlangga then assumed responsibility for the unruly river and undertook a royal project to construct dams at strategic points on the Brantas. These dams reduced the danger of floods and enhanced the possibilities for irrigation. Some sources further suggest that Airlangga subsequently transferred farming populations from Central to East Java to fill up the delta. His water control project also improved the harbor at the royal port of Hujung Galah to better serve a growing international trade (K. Hall, 1985a: 129–34, 301).

Soon thereafter East Java became the most important center in the maritime realm and the home of an international spice market that served much of the Eastern Hemisphere. Indeed, from the eleventh to the fifteenth century the East Javanese had what was tantamount to a monopoly over the fine spices (cloves, nutmeg, and mace). The Spice Islanders—the inhabitants of the Moluccas, who tended the trees and harvested and processed the spices—were still the only people in the world who could produce these spices in commercial quantities. The Malay sailors who shipped the spices thus transported expensive cargoes. These they brought to the harbors of East Java, where they could purchase the goods, including ordinary foodstuffs, that the Spice Islanders needed or wanted.

In a way, the winds also conspired to protect East Java's position as the sole supplier of the fine spices, for they made it quite unlikely that international traders would ever encounter either the producers or the sailors who delivered the spices to East Java's ports. Ships laden with cloves, nutmeg, and mace came to Java on the same monsoon winds that international traders used to return to India or China; the spice carriers made their way back to the Moluccas on the same winds that delivered the international traders to Java. Thus, while traders from outside the maritime realm were in Java, the ships that carried the spices were in the Moluccas, and once the international traders had left for their destinations, the ships would arrive from the Moluccas with the spices. In addition, the monsoon pattern may well have contributed to the mistaken notion that the spices were produced locally since traders were unlikely to witness the arrival of these cargoes in port.

Airlangga took a percentage of all the valuable metals, such as gold, silver, or copper, used by foreign merchants to make purchases in the markets. He also supervised the provision of services to foreign merchants, ensuring the adequacy of the harbor, the board and lodging of the visitors, and the safe storage of their goods. The royal revenues were used to pay soldiers and sailors who acted in the monarch's name to force the subjugation of ambitious locales that threatened his center's predominance. These men also policed the realm, eliminating pirates and bandits that might prey on travelers or villagers. The security thus provided was essential to the commercial well-being of East Java, for otherwise international traders might avoid the region. The Chinese, for example, were aware that pepper was available for a good price in the vicinity of the Sunda Strait, but did not choose to go there since it had a reputation for brigandage (K. Hall, 1985a: 341, n. 52).

## The Expansion of Royal Prerogatives by Charter

Airlangga's activism, which was required in order to overcome the disadvantages of the Brantas river basin, also resulted in a significant increase in the power and prerogatives of the royal center, accompanied by an erosion of the traditional rights of local landed elites. To this end, Airlangga followed precedents set by East Javanese kings of the previous century, who had used royal charters to establish a direct link between themselves and local rulers who wished to promote their ports and populate their lands. These charters were essentially agreements, carved in stone or engraved on metal plaques, spelling out the conditions of what was essentially a contract between the king and the local persons or groups named in the charter.

Airlangga used these charters to create a direct relationship, unmediated by the local elites, between himself and the merchants of the Brantas river basin. These merchants, who generally lived in the ports, carried goods of foreign origin (such things as metals and dyes) to local village markets. There they bought rice and other foodstuffs, transporting them back to the ports. The charters that Airlangga issued to them essentially turned the merchants into royal tax collectors, a role that had previously been played by outsiders (Wisseman, 1977: 206–7).

## Aesthetics and Power

Airlangga and the East Javanese kings who succeeded him also used a portion of their revenues to provide patronage to scholars, build temples and monuments, and perform ceremonies—all designed to impress upon an audience the monarch's superior status and the prestige of his capital. Often, however, it was far from the central area, albeit usually in localities of strategic importance, that the monuments were built or the ceremonies held, since the king would graciously remit a part of a given locality's obligations to the center in return for their celebration of his greatness at the local level. In addition, the king's position was enhanced by the strategic gift-giving that took place during ceremonies at the center.

One mark of a group's access to the center, a source of prestige and power at the local level, was the possession of rare, imported goods that the king bestowed on the worthy. Chinese porcelain may well have been one of the items that served this purpose in the early centuries of East Java's hegemony. Porcelain was never mentioned in the lists of market goods found on inscriptions, and yet Chinese records indicate that significant quantities of porcelain were shipped to Java around this time, and numerous ceramic shards have been recovered from this period (Wisseman-Christie, 1991: 37).

Although Buddhism did not disappear, there was a resurgence of Hindu gods and goddesses (a trend that had also characterized the latter part of Central Java's temple boom), as well as a melding of both religions with elements of indigenous Javanese systems of belief (D. Hall, 1968: 67–70). By the tenth century Javanese had become a written language (for which the Sanskrit script was employed), and portions of the Hindu epics, the *Mahabharata* and the *Ramayana,* has been translated into Javanese. Inscriptions were no longer written in Sanskrit but in the local language, and the names of foreign priests no longer appear on them (Wisseman-Christie, 1983: 25, 27). Javanese law was also codified, transforming the various local traditions into a uniform system (D. Hall, 1968: 67).

A written Javanese literature, in prose and poetry, also emerged around the time of Airlangga's reign. Perhaps the best-known piece from this early period is the *Arjuna Wiwaha* (The marriage of Arjuna) (D. Hall, 1968: 70; Coedès, 1968: 147), an epic poem about a hero of the *Mahabharata.* Nevertheless, the author, the court poet Kanwa, was clearly inspired by Javanese concerns and wrote for Javanese sensibilities. At the climax of the poem is a scene in which Arjuna meditates, intent upon concentrating the powers of his mind on the defeat of his enemies. Even seductive nymphs, sent by his enemies to distract him from this purpose, are unable to break his concentration. This image captured the imagination of Airlangga's eulogizer, who subsequently portrayed the king as possessing the same powers of meditation when he was fighting with "demons" in Central Java.

East Java also produced an art that was distinctly different, both from the art of India and that of Central Java (Soekmono, 1971: 13–17). Sculptures of the Buddha and bodhisattvas receded into the background, full-bodied images of Javanese rulers coming instead to the fore. Indigenous symbols and images of power, often in the form of real or imagined animals, proliferated, many fashioned in larger than human proportion. For example, an eleventh-century statue of Airlangga, originally erected beside his grave at the Bath of Belehan and now in the museum in Majakarta, portrays the monarch as an earthly manifestation of Visnu, the Hindu Lord God who, in the guise of Krishna, urged Arjuna to take up arms against those who had wrongfully seized power. (See illustration 15, p. 63). The statue depicts Airlangga on Visnu's mount, the man-bird Garuda, who is almost twice the size of the king. Local artists were fascinated by Garuda, the sun-linked vanquisher of the serpent, and Javanese sculptors have produced some of the world's most imposing visions of this carrier of the gods. (Even today, when 89 percent of its population is Muslim, Garuda is the national symbol of Indonesia and the name of its national airline.)

**The Realm Divided**

After Airlangga's death in 1049, his descendants were unable to hold up the great umbrella that he had raised, with the result that the constituent parts of Airlangga's realm reemerged as autonomous kingdoms (Kulke, 1991: 17). In later Javanese literature, this period of local autonomy was understood to be the result of an actual division into two parts of a truly integrated empire. In the east, upriver, was Janggala/Singasari, and on the middle and lower reaches of the Brantas, Kediri. Contemporary scholars now believe that these locales had never been obliterated and incorporated into Airlangga's realm, and thus there was no division *per se*. (Nevertheless, some two hundred years later, Airlangga's umbrella-like sovereignty was remembered as real enough to justify the unification of these locales under the kings of Singasari [Kulke, 1986: 15–16].) There is, however, no indication that East Java's commercial position was damaged by political fragmentation. Taxable goods traded in Javanese markets during this time included "tin from Malaya, copper from China and mainland Southeast Asia, iron from sources perhaps as distant as the East African coast, silver perhaps from Burma, and gold from many sources" (Wisseman-Christie, 1991: 36). Other important items of trade included dyestuffs from the forests of other maritime realm islands, silks and cast-iron consumer goods from China, cotton from Bali and the lowlands of eastern Java, and other local goods such as salt, salted fish, and pottery.

Compelling testimony regarding Java's commercial appeal during this period comes from Zhao Rugua, Commissioner of Foreign Trade at the Chinese port of Quanzhou. Gold and silver coins, which were minted in Java, were universally used to pay taxes and debts "and to purchase everything from cloth and buffaloes to land and buildings," and Chinese copper cash also had become an acceptable currency on the island (Wisseman-Christie, 1991: 37). In his study of international trade, dated 1225, Zhao indicates that Chinese merchants were using these copper coins minted by the Chinese government to purchase spices and other goods in eastern Javanese markets. So popular were these goods, in fact, that the copper coins were flowing out of the empire at a rate that alarmed the Chinese government.

# 6 SINGASARI *(1222 to 1292)* AND MAJAPAHIT *(1292 to 1528)*

## Consolidation and Expansion in the Age of the Mongols

The Mongols were Central Asian nomads whose homeland was many thousands of miles away from the maritime realm. Nevertheless, their activities form a backdrop to the history of Southeast Asia in the thirteenth and fourteenth centuries. Forged into an army of conquest by Genghis Khan (1162–1227), the Mongols spent the thirteenth century conquering or invading almost all of Asia and eastern Europe. In much of Asia this century was consequently marked by the destruction of venerable centers of power, although for East Java this was a period of consolidation and expansion.

In the year 1222 the ruler of Singasari, Ken Androk, subjugated Kediri and thereby reunited East Java, which is to say that once again and for the first time since the death of Airlangga, a single umbrella of sovereignty was raised over the realm. Shortly thereafter, during the reign of King Visnuvaidhana (1248–1268) a new, highly syncretic worldview emerged, fusing elements from several local and Indian traditions. Fittingly, when Visnuvaidhana died his ashes were divided between two shrines. At one he was worshiped as an incarnation of Siva, and at the other as Amoghapusa, the Bodhisattva of Compassion. His son, the mysterious and controversial Kertanagara (r. 1268–1292), claimed to have been initiated into secret Tantric rites that gave him extraordinary powers against demonic forces. He came to the throne only after destroying "a wicked man" and subsequently carried out what he characterized as a religious revival of the realm. That he saw a relationship between political unification and spiritual revival is clear from the placement of a statue he commissioned, in which he is depicted as Aksubhya, the meditative Buddha: he erected it on the very spot where Bharada (the Hindu ascetic blamed for the partition of Airlangga's realm) had lived (Slametmuljana, 1976: 26).

In order to maintain his phenomenal powers, Kertanagara was obliged to go into ecstatic trances inspired by Tantric rituals that required the consumption of intoxicating drink and the performance of sexual acts. This created much controversy, both at the time and later on. The *Nagarakertagama,* a Javanese epic composed in 1365 by the Tantric Buddhist monk Prapanca, assures one and all that Kertanagara was a saint and ascetic, free of all passions. But a fifteenth-century chronicler, hostile to Tantric rituals, was not convinced, portraying Kertanagara in the *Pararatan* as a drunkard who was brought to ruin by his lust (K. Hall, 1985a: 251).

There is, however, no controversy regarding Kertanagara's political significance. Against the Eurasianwide backdrop of the Mongol conquests, he laid the foundations for an empire of grand proportions. By the time that Kertanagara came to power in 1268, northern China had long been held by the Mongols, and parts of mainland Southeast Asia and southern China had already been invaded. The Thais had also taken this opportunity to expand, infringing upon what had been Burmese Pagan to the west, Cambodian Angkor to the east, and the Malay Peninsula to the south. Then in 1274 the Mongols attempted their first overseas invasion, launching an attack against Japan. Kertanagara apparently was alarmed by these developments, especially by Thai expansion into the maritime realm, and in 1275 he sent an expedition to occupy the Sumatran port of Jambi-Malayu.

In 1271, Khubulai Khan (1215–1294), the grandson of Genghis, announced the establishment of the Yuan dynasty (some eight years before he completed his conquest of China's Southern Song dynasty). Soon thereafter, various ports in or near the Strait of Malacca responded to this shift in China's heavenly mandate by applying for commercial relations with its new Mongolian rulers. In 1277 Palembang, in 1281 Jambi-Malayu, and in 1282 Samudra-Pasai (a pepper depot on the northern tip of Sumatra) sent envoys to Khubulai's capital. But Kertanagara had no intention of letting these ports reestablish the power that Srivijaya had once possessed. After subjugating Bali in 1284, he sent his armies westward, and by 1286 he had established Javanese hegemony over the straits region. To mark his preeminence, he erected a statue of his father at Jambi-Malayu. His father was portrayed as Amoghapusa, the Bodhisattva of Compassion, and the inscription indicated that it was dedicated to the joy of all Kertanagara's subjects (K. Hall, 1985a: 251).

Khubulai Khan was not pleased by Singasari's policies of expansion. In 1289 he sent envoys to Kertanagara's court, demanding that East Java submit to his will and send a tribute mission to his capital. Kertanagara replied by disfiguring the faces of the envoys and then sending them home in this disgraced fashion. In retaliation Khubulai Khan sent a thousand warships to chastise Singasari and its ruler, but before the fleet arrived, Kertanagara was murdered in the last months of 1292 by a local rival ruler in Kediri. After this calamity, Kertanagara's son-in-law, Raden Vijaya (sometimes written Wijaya), became king. Abandoning the upland center at Singasari, he cleared a site for a new capital on the Brantas delta. When the Mongol warships arrived in 1293, intent upon the punishment of Singasari, Raden Vijaya cleverly informed them that the offending kingdom had fallen and that its ruler had been murdered. He then persuaded the Mongols to join him in a punitive expedition in order to chastise the "murderers," with the result that he was able to destroy his local enemies, with Mongolian assistance. That accomplished, he turned on the Mongols, defeated them, and forced them out of Java (Slametmuljana, 1976: 43–44).

The new capital that King Vijaya founded in 1292 was to be known as Majapahit. It was located about 25 miles upriver from the Brantas delta port of Surabaya, a little to the southeast of present-day Majakerta (near where Airlangga's capital may have been) (Slametmuljana, 1976: 40, 132). It would soon become the grandest realm that maritime Southeast Asia had yet seen, its kings possessing an unprecedented degree of central control over East Java (Kulke, 1991: 19). These kings would also subordinate Bali and Central Java, thereby establishing hegemony over an overseas realm almost three times the size of Srivijaya's. To mass a navy with which to secure its control over this far-flung realm, Majapahit employed a tactic similar to that used by Srivijaya: seafaring peoples based in ports on Java's north coast were rewarded by the monarchs for their good behavior and their services.

**Expansion of the International Market**

Khubulai Khan died soon after the Javanese victory over the Mongolian expedition of 1293. His successor as emperor of the Yuan dynasty did not share his overseas ambitions and thus abandoned the attempt to subjugate Java and Japan. Peace was restored and commercial relations with China were reestablished. At the same time, developments at the opposite end of the hemisphere, in western Europe, further expanded the market for the spices that East Java distributed. After undergoing an agricultural and commercial revolution and leading crusades in the eastern Mediterranean for some two hundred years, western Europeans had begun to consume meat in quantity. They had therefore developed a taste for South Asian spices, which were ideal for flavoring dried, salted, or merely stale meat, as well as for preserving vegetables and fruits.

Venice was the principal supplier of the expanding European market. The Italian city-state would take over much of Byzantium's Mediterranean trade, while Genoa developed a new sea route to Portugal, Flanders, and England. Eventually Venice achieved what was tantamount to a monopoly over the spice market in western Europe (Abu-Lughod, 1989: 215; Simkin, 1968: 175). Owing to the Mongol conquests of the lands of the Abbasid Caliphate in the first half of the thirteenth century, Venetian merchants, such as the family of Marco Polo, were able to travel through the Middle East, from Europe to China. The most important suppliers of Venetian merchants, however, were still found in the ports of Egypt, thanks to the Mamluk rulers of Egypt (1250–1511). The Mamluks had defeated the Mongols before they reached Egypt and had once again secured the Red Sea route from the Indian Ocean to the Mediterranean.

Nor were the Mamluks forced to live without gold. During the first half of the thirteenth century, Sundiata, the founder of the Empire of Mali, had united much of the West African savannah, and his successors established close relations with the Mamluks. Thus, the stream of West African gold into Egypt grew ever broader. Mali's gold also went to North African ports west of Egypt, albeit in lesser amounts, making it possible for cities in southern France and Italy to obtain African gold and mint their own gold coins.

The realm of Majapahit would meet this expanded demand, and it would be changed in the process. Java's own marketing network benefited from the growth in international demand, the internal peace and security provided by Majapahit's hegemony, the growing concentration of nonagrarian populations (merchants, artisans, and government officials) in urban centers and towns, and from royal efforts to remove obstacles between hinterland producers and ports. The relationship between Majapahit's kings and its merchants grew so close that some sources, both local and foreign, considered Java's spice merchants to be little more than the monarch's agents of trade. Although this was an exaggeration, it was certainly true that the kings received a share of the port's revenues, controlled the bullion and luxury goods that flowed in, and received a share of the profits made from the exchange and transportation of local and international products.

## The Realm and Its Ceremony

By 1331 the kings at Majapahit had secured all of eastern Java as well as the island of Madura, placing their own relatives at the head of each of the kingdom's divisions. By 1343 Bali had been secured and was thereafter ruled by Javanese princes. In 1347 the kings began subordinating ports to their north and east, a process that culminated with their ritual hegemony over places as far away as the southern Philippines and New Guinea. Although Majapahit had on occasion punished local rulers in the straits region who became too ambitious—as did one ruler in the Sunda Strait in 1357—it apparently felt no need to establish a regular presence there until 1377. This change of attitude may have been prompted by a Sumatran response to yet another shift in China's heavenly mandate. In 1368 Chinese rebels expelled the Mongol Yuan dynasty and established a new dynasty, the Ming. China's new rulers immediately invited Palembang to send a tribute mission to their capital at Nanjing, and the Sumatrans duly arrived in 1371. Apparently, though, Majapahit's rulers feared that a strong relationship between China and the straits region would allow the latter to regain the preeminent position that it had enjoyed in the days of Srivijaya. East Java's 1377 expedition against this ambitious Sumatran port evidently succeeded, for soon thereafter representatives of the ports in the straits region were participating in the central ceremonies of Majapahit (K. Hall, 1985a: 248).

Even Samudra-Pasai, a pepper depot located on the far side of the Strait of Malacca, on the northern end of Sumatra, was an enthusiastic participant in the ceremonial realm of Majapahit. One of its chroniclers remembered the eastern Java center at its height:

> The [Majapahit] Emperor was famous for his love of justice. The empire grew prosperous. People in vast numbers thronged the city. At this

time every kind of food was in great abundance. There was a ceaseless coming and going of people from the territories overseas which had submitted to the king, to say nothing of places inside Java itself. Of the districts on the coast, from the west came the whole of the west, from the east came the whole of the east. From places inland right down to the shores of the Southern Ocean the people all came for an audience with the Emperor, bringing tribute and offerings. . . . The land of Majapahit was supporting a large population. Everywhere one went there were gongs and drums being beaten, people dancing to the strains of all kinds of loud music, entertainments of many kinds like the living theater, the shadow play, masked-plays, step-dancing and musical dramas. These were the commonest sights and went on day and night in the land of Majapahit. (Hill, 1960: 161, cited in K. Hall, 1985a: 340, n. 47)

Travelers who came to Majapahit in the latter part of the fourteenth century, at the peak of its glory, approached on a merchant ship and entered the core area of the realm at the port of Surabaya, a town of about a thousand households (including some that were Chinese). To reach the center of Majapahit they then took a small boat up the Brantas River, through the flat and fertile delta region. After going about 25 miles upstream they arrived at Canggu, a ferry crossing and a market-place, walking south from there to the "twin cities," Bubat and Majapahit. Majapahit was the royal center, but visitors arrived first at Bubat, a market town located on a wide plain immediately north of the capital (K. Hall, 1985a: 235; Slametmuljana, 1976: 40).

Most foreigners stayed at Bubat, a cosmopolitan town boasting many quarters, of which the Chinese and the Indian were the largest. The market was located in a large square, surrounded on three sides by tall and splendid buildings, paneled with carvings of scenes from the *Mahabharata*. Java's own traders brought their goods here, and local artisans offered their wares. Merchants from many lands, including India, China, Cambodia, Vietnam, and Thailand, gathered here to do their trading as well (K. Hall, 1985a: 246–47).

Because of its close relationship to the royal capital, Bubat acquired some of the attributes of a ritual center. Every spring, at some point in March or April, it was the site of the Caitra festival, a celebration of the first fruits of the season and a veneration of the rice goddess Sri (van Setten van der Meer, 1979: 113). The festival involved a succession of ceremonies designed to display Majapahit's political and social relationships and economic capabilities. After initial rituals at the royal center, in which both Hindu Brahmins and Buddhist monks prayed for the royal house's prosperity, the court "came down" for the first seven days of the festival. The princes paraded in golden attire and Brahmins offered the king holy water in finely made pitchers. The scholars, nobles, and judges of the realm moved in stately procession to the beat of ceremonial drums and the blare of conch shells and trumpets, while singers and poets sang the praises of Majapahit.

At Bubat both the court and the visitors could enjoy all that was offered, the music, dancing, and drama, along with games, gambling, and trials of combat. From special viewing stands the royal personages and their honored guests—holy men, allies from within the realm, and foreign visitors from many lands—watched as the Javanese fought with weapons, or demonstrated their skills at unarmed combat, or engaged in an elaborate tug-of-war.

Then the principal ceremonies began. First the king received various collections in kind and in cash. The court's right to a share of the local specialties produced throughout the realm ensured his supply of rice, salt, sugar, salted meats, cloth, oil, and bamboo. International traders brought gifts for the king as well, and thus he amassed a mountain of goods. But he could not hoard them. A king was measured by his generosity, and so he was expected to redistribute the bounty among those present. He bestowed gifts upon the artisans (such as those who had built the viewing stands) in return for the labor and materials that they had contributed. Gifts were also given to the musicians and poets and other performers who had contributed to the festival's success, while other goods would be consumed at the feasts that ended the festivities. In addition, a portion of local and imported luxury items (such as silk and porcelain) would be distributed to the king's allies, and thereby dispersed throughout the realm. It was the king's wealth and power that created his prestige and attracted his tributaries to him, but they expected something in return, something they deemed equal to their own importance. At the close of the ceremonies, as the moon of the spring month of Caitra waned, the court received the representatives of common village communities. These, too, went away with presents of clothing and food.

The seven days of celebrations at Bubat were followed by seven more days of festivities at Majapahit's royal center. Here the royal family and its allies, including local land-based elites, gathered for further ceremonies and speeches. One theme was the importance of the farmers and the royal military. Neither the royal house nor the market towns could survive without the produce of the villages. Java's international position was, moreover, ultimately based on its rice, the major commodity sought by the harvesters of spice. It was for rice that they came to Java, and so the livelihood of the farmers had to be protected. Likewise, prosperity would be impossible without the security provided by the military (Pigeaud, 1960: 3:101–5). That the commercial elite recognized the importance of the king's military is indicated by the generous contributions (8,000 copper cash per day) that market heads made to the commander-in-chief of Majapahit's forces (K. Hall, 1985a: 247).

The ceremonies culminated in a community meal that once again marked out the relationships between the center and its allies. Those closest to the royal line were served on gold plates and ate their fill of mutton, water buffalo, poultry, game, wild boar, bees, fish, and ducks. Those of lesser rank and relationship, including the commoners, were served on silver dishes and were offered "meats innumerable, all there is on the land and in the water," including those that the high-ranking did not eat—frog, worm, tortoise, mouse, and dog (Pigeaud, 1960: 3:106). Along with this food came prodigious quantities of alcoholic beverages made from the fruits of various varieties of palm trees, from sugar, and from rice. One and all drank until they were drunk, "panting, vomiting, or bewildered" (Pigeaud, 1960: 3:107).

The food and drink were, in turn, accompanied by the best in entertainment, including singers and dancers and a musical play in which the princes of the realm and the king himself acted and sang. According to a court bard, these royal players were a hit:

> Merriness made the beginning; without interruption was the laughing together in succession,
>
> and pity aroused weeping, giving anguish, causing tears,
>
> Therefore those who saw it were altogether touched in their minds.
>
> The inclination of the sun was declining: then the Prince was making an end.
>
> Then the common . . . [village leaders] took their leave, wiping our lord's Foot-soles.

The words of those . . . [village leaders] were: released from evil, given
joy as if not in the world.

Not to be mentioned is their praise. Our lord at last returned into the
Interior. (Pigeaud, 1960: 3:109).

## The Expansion of Royal Power

In the 1330s, shortly before the kings of Majapahit began to consolidate their far-flung maritime empire, they also began to consolidate the
royal center's control over the resources and the people of eastern
Java. The two processes of expansion and centralization were almost
simultaneous. The trend toward centralization within the Brantas river
basin can be traced back to the tenth century, when the early kings had
used port merchants and foreigners as royal "tax farmers" to ensure
that hinterland rice reached the royal port. Airlangga had carried the
process a step further when he dammed the Brantas River and thereby
gained some degree of leverage over local agricultural elites, who
depended on the river's water for irrigation. Apparently Airlangga also
dispensed with the use of foreigners as tax farmers, preferring to rely
on local port merchants to collect his share from the villages. Then,
during the Majapahit period, even the tax farmers were eliminated.
Payments of rice due to the royal government were instead collected
by state ministers within the royal domains, while local allies were
obliged to deliver their own part of the king's share directly to him.

But even in times of centralization, the king's supply of agricultural
produce came largely from his own domains, the amount of tribute rice
expected from allies remaining small. For the most part, rice from
outside the royal domain continued to move to Java's ports through
market mechanisms, rather than to the royal center by taxation or
tribute. Because of their income from the commercial sector, it was not
necessary for Majapahit's monarchs to challenge the foundation of
local autonomy and prosperity by increasing their collection of agricultural produce from their subordinated allies. To increase its demands
on the agrarian sector the state would have had to infringe further upon
the most basic political rights and socioeconomic powers of the entrenched local elites. Thus, when kings sought to enhance royal revenue and authority, they did not pursue a larger share of the realm's
agricultural resources. Instead they sought greater control over the

wealth generated outside of the agricultural sector. They were content to tax local commerce and nonagricultural production, to promote the cause of merchants and artisans who could best assist in facilitating the flow of goods to and from Java's north coast ports, and in general, to encourage the development of Java's economy.

Speeches made during the Caitra festival by princes at the royal center also made clear the significance of public works and transportation networks. Such speakers addressed the necessity of maintaining public works that were under government protection, such as dams, bridges, fountains, and marketplaces, together with projects such as tree planting. Some of these public structures were built and maintained by the center; others were the responsibility of local elites, although their neglect would not go unnoticed by the center. Also among the royal projects were roads that linked the capital to important places. The roads generally ran perpendicular to the rivers and thus intersected with them, and wherever they did so there were ferries large enough to move carts across the rivers. One authority estimates that there may have been as many as 150 ferry crossings in the coastal region on the deltas of the Brantas and Solo Rivers alone (Wisseman-Christie, 1991: 29).

The ruler and his retinue periodically traveled along this road network, making the royal rounds to receive the homage of the various subordinates. At each stop the king performed ceremonies that the local elite had to pay for (an indirect form of taxation). Payments for goods and services used by the royal procession were, however, made to local merchants and artisans, so these expenses did not involve a transfer of revenues out of the district. Merchants and tradesmen also used these roads, and their traveling markets are well represented in scenes carved on temple walls during the Majapahit era (K. Hall, 1985a: 234–35). The *Nagarakertagama* speaks of "caravans of carts" and crowded highways, and even of cart accidents during the rainier months from October to February: "The road . . . over the whole length then was difficult, narrow. There followed rains. The incline being altogether slippery, several carts were damaged there, colliding one with another" (Pigeaud, 1960: 3:29). Consequently, during the rainy season most goods were moved by boat on the rivers.

One of the principal means by which the king enriched the royal treasury and enhanced royal power was to issue royal charters that created a more direct relationship between the court and various groups of taxpayers within the eastern Java core of the realm. These charters reveal an accelerating trend toward relieving specified people of their former obligations to local land-based elites by transferring them into the role of royal tax payers. As a result, such people gained a new and direct relationship with the king and the court. These charters thus deprived the local authorities of some of their nonagricultural revenue as well as some of their control over nonagricultural populations.

Prior to the Canggu Ferry Charter of 1358, the people who operated the ferries had no relationship with the royal court. Rather, they had been viewed as constituents of the local landed elites and had accordingly paid their taxes to them. Under the new charter, however, they were no longer obliged to pay taxes or tribute to local authorities but were instead required to deliver a quantity of textiles directly to the king and to make a substantial contribution of flowers and cash to help pay for royal ceremonies. In particular, the charter required them to make a contribution of goods and money for Bubat's Caitra festival, a contribution that entitled them to participate in the celebration along with the royal family, local lineages, and distinguished guests. This was an unprecedented recognition—indeed, an overt display—of their economic and military importance as facilitators of transportation in eastern Java.

Three charters, dated 1336, 1391, and 1395, concerned the markets in two neighboring towns, Bililuk and Tanggulnam. Their contents paint a picture of bustling towns in the highlands of the interior, where the people engaged in salt manufacture (from saline streams), sugar refining, water buffalo meat packing, oil pressing, and rice noodle manufacturing. The charters further reveal the presence of textile workers, who bought cloth and dyes in the market. Most likely they were producing batiks, a specialty of Southeast Asia. The market also offered four kinds of spices (which may have been used in quantity by the meat packers), iron implements, ceramics, rattan, and cloth.

Prior to the granting of royal charters, the artisans and merchants in a given region had been subject to a local chief of trade, a representative of the landed elite who supervised the market and to whom they had been obliged to make contributions on at least thirteen different occasions. One obligation concerned contributions toward his travel and transport costs, while five others pertained to births, marriages, or deaths in his family. The remaining seven involved contributions toward the entertaining of special guests. The chief of trade, in turn, had been at the mercy of the king's port-based tax farmers, whose demands were equally arbitrary and unpredictable. The royal charters granted to Bililuk and Tanggulnam abolished the various and assorted obligations that these people had previously owed to the chief of trade. In their place was instituted a direct and fixed tax that they owed to the king, which the king then shared with the chief of trade.

Other royal charters issued to communities in eastern Java required that local resources be applied toward the performance of ceremonies at the local level that honored the monarch and displayed his powers. In addition, they often provided that a portion of the resources due to the king be designated as contributions to royal ritual at the capital, in which representatives of the local community were required to participate. Some charters also specified that a certain percentage of the new royal taxes should be paid with copper cash, one indication of increasing monetarization of the economy (K. Hall, 1985a: 236–42).

## Literature and Art

By the time of Majapahit, Java's native stories had begun to appear in written form and to be the subjects of sculpture. One epic glorified Majapahit's victory in 1357 over a king of the Sunda Strait, while another, the *Tjalon Arang,* was set in Airlangga's reign and told the story of a struggle between the Hindu holy man Bharada and a witch armed with black magic. The saga of Damar Wulan concerned a prince to whom fate dealt a series of cruel blows but who in the end won a kingdom. Perhaps most enjoyed were the stories of Pandji, whose beautiful fiancée was stolen from him, to be recovered only after many adventures (Mau Vetter, 1984: 32).

A new style of art also emerged in the thirteenth century, in which the beatific and tranquil spirit of earlier sculpture gave way to a more robust and challenging attitude. Many temples were built, as well, although they usually were not as large as those constructed during Central Java's earlier temple boom. Nor were they as orthodox. Borobudur is clearly Buddhist, and Prambanan Hindu, but these temples, like the kings who were their patrons, were syncretic in outlook, blending a number of religious traditions into one. Their walls were covered with carvings so ornate and so profusely filled with people and things that one art historian has characterized the style as "flamboyant baroque" (Holt, 1967: 87). The figures on the panels of the temples and other monuments were no longer as round, becoming almost two-dimensional, like *wayang* puppets. Beasts proliferated, including a multitude of ferocious-looking creatures that would make the *kala* heads at Borobudur pale by comparison. All who saw them knew to approach with reverence.

Majapahit's power was reaching its high tide by the end of the fourteenth century, a tide that brought with it a culmination of all the traditions, indigenous and incorporated through Southeast Asia's participation in the Hindu and Buddhist worlds. However, as the fifteenth century dawned so did a number of developments that would eventually undermine the power and prestige of the Majapahit court and eastern Java's preeminence in relationship to Central Java and the straits region. By the sixteenth century Java's most powerful political center would reside once again on the volcanic plains of Central Java—the site of the eighth- to tenth-century temple boom, commercial ascendancy would gravitate back to the straits region, and the majority of the population within Southeast Asia's maritime realm were becoming participants in an even larger Muslim world. None of these changes came about rapidly. Eastern Java's centrality within the maritime world had been long in the making, dating back at least to the eleventh-century reign of Airlangga, and its dissolution, not surprisingly, was also a long process that took more than a century.

# 7 THE ESTABLISHMENT OF MUSLIM MATARAM

The forces that brought an end to Majapahit, and to eastern Java's hegemony over the island realm, were both subtle and large. One might even argue that Majapahit's main problem was that it was simply too successful. Although the growth of its international spice market contributed to the region's commercial and political preeminence from the eleventh to the fifteenth century, the further development of that same market contributed to its decline. The market became so large, and it offered so many opportunities, that Majapahit could not control it indefinitely. As coastal trading communities prospered both within and beyond the realm, the ports over which Majapahit held sway became increasingly independent. The conversion to Islam of Java's own commercial communities signaled this growing independence—and a reconfiguration of international trading patterns as well.

By 1400 Majapahit was losing control over the more distant parts of its realm and over the business in spice. One indication of its weakness was the increase in piracy in the straits region, which prompted Chinese naval expeditions to step in to ensure the safe passage of ships through the Strait of Malacca. In so doing, they contributed to the emergence of a new straits power at Malacca, which in turn drew the Malay sailors with their spices and thus the international traders in unprecedented numbers. In the end, Majapahit was defeated by townspeople, indigenous to its northern coast, who had become Muslims. The victors moved the royal center from eastern Java back to Central Java, to Jogjakarta, establishing a kingdom known as Mataram.

## Conversion to Islam

The Muslim challengers who overthrew Majapahit and established a new Muslim Mataram were not foreigners, but Javanese who had converted to Islam. Although Muslims from the Middle Eastern caliphates had been present in Southeast Asia ever since the founding of Islam, there were few conversions there before the end of the thirteenth century. It was only after the Mongol and Turkic conquests on the Eurasian landmass and the subsequent spread of Sufi mysticism that Islam began to attract large numbers of converts in the maritime realm.

Maritime Southeast Asia's conversion to Islam was thus part of a more general expansion of the Prophet's religion that accompanied an epoch of Turko-Mongolian hegemony, roughly from 1200 to 1600. Islam had become well established in Iran and in the Persian-speaking regions of Central Asia during the time of the Abbasid Caliphate. After the caliphate began to recruit Turkish nomads from Central Asia to man its armies, Turkish populations on the steppe also began converting to Islam. Beginning in the tenth century, after the power of the Abbasids had weakened, a resurgence of local power and local culture took place in Iran, a development known as the New Persian Renaissance. Although the Iranians remained Muslim, there was a rebirth of pre-Islamic traditions (believed to have characterized the Zoroastrian-influenced Achaemenid and Sassanian periods) in literature, art, and historical studies. The Turkish powers that ruled much of eastern Iran and adjacent parts of Central Asia were enthusiastic participants in these cultural developments. They sponsored a new Turkish culture, an eclectic blend of Turkic steppe traditions and the New Persian culture.

When the Mongols conquered both Central Asia and Iran in the early thirteenth century, they still served ancestral and natural spirits, rather than adhering to any of the scriptured religions. However, by the end of the century the descendants of the conquerors living in the area of the Iranian and Turkish renaissances had become Muslims and had begun to forge a new Turko-Mongolian culture, a creative mix of Persian, Turkic, and Mongolian traditions. By the fourteenth century, poetry, architecture, and art, including a new style of miniature painting, were flourishing, and this new culture had begun to spread along with the expansion of Turkish and Turko-Mongolian powers. The Ottomans in the Anatolian region, the Mamluks in Egypt, the Timurids in Central Asia, the Safavids in Iran, and the Mughals in India were all promoters of this new culture. Ultimately these powers would hold sway from North Africa to southern India, and from the Black Sea to the borders of China.

The group from this Turko-Mongolian region most responsible for the spread of Islam to Southeast Asia during this period were the Sufis, mystics who sought ways to a personal communion with Allah. Islam in Central Asia had a strong mystical element from its inception, and after the Mongol conquests, Sufism became an integral part of the new Turko-Mongolian culture. By the end of the thirteenth century, Sufi saints were traveling over the same roads and on the same ships as Muslim merchants, and their spiritual powers were attracting the attention of many Africans and Southeast Asians.

The first place within the realm of Majapahit to become Muslim was Samudra-Pasai, a small polity in northern Sumatra that controlled both a pepper-producing hinterland and a coastal port. Near the end of the thirteenth century, at more or less the same time that Majapahit was founded, Merah Silu, the aspiring leader of Samudra-Pasai, converted to the faith of the Prophet. He had first established his military and economic legitimacy in the hinterland near the headwaters of the Pasangan River, and it was from this base that he conquered the coast. Thereafter, according to local tradition, he was converted to Islam not by any foreigner traveler but by the Prophet Mohammed himself, who came to Merah Silu in a dream. The Prophet gave him the name Malik al-Salih, and when he awoke he could recite the Koran and the Islamic confession of faith.

Some forty days later, as Mohammed had prophesied in the dream, a ship arrived from Mecca carrying a Muslim holy man as well as a sultan from Malabar (India's pepper coast) (K. Hall, 1977: 217–18). Although this tradition suggests that it was a connection with India's Malabar coast that led to the conversion of Samudra-Pasai, it appears that Islam in fact came to Southeast Asia from various parts of India. Some scholars believe that it spread from ports in the vicinity of Gujarat, after Turkish conquerors became established there in 1297 (Slametmuljana, 1976: 205, 223), while others have suggested several additional sources in southern India, including the Coromandel coast (K. Hall, 1977: 218).

During the fourteenth century Samudra-Pasai became a center of Islamic studies, the first within the island realm, although for the first hundred years of its existence neither this port nor the gradual spread of Islam to other ports had much impact on Majapahit's power. During this same century when Majapahit was extending its dominion out over the seas, the representatives of Muslim Samudra-Pasai numbered among the loyal participants in the center's ceremonies. However, by the end of the century, Muslim merchant communities could be found throughout the maritime realm, and even some members of Majapahit's royal family had converted. It was only at this point that Islam became a cause around which dissatisfaction with the eastern Javanese center could coalesce. Majapahit's power and prestige were gone, and some of its constituent parts felt that it no longer served "their" interests. In particular, the ports on Java's northern coast began to resent its claims upon them—whereas Islam offered both a new faith and a new sense of community. It thus provided a rationale for rejecting the special claims of aristocratic lineage and the special religious connections upon which Majapahit's legitimacy had rested.

**The Port of Malacca**

Majapahit's decline in the fifteenth century was paralleled by the growth of Malacca, a new port on the strait that now bears its name. It was established in 1402 by Paramesvara, a Sumatran prince who claimed descent from the royal lineage associated with Palembang, once the center of Srivijaya. This was not the prince's first attempt to establish a port in the straits region, but previously Thai forces had managed to block any efforts on his part to settle on or near the Malay Peninsula (Coedès, 1968: 245). Majapahit, too, had been hostile to such attempts, but now it was preoccupied with problems at its very core and was therefore in no position to interfere. The years 1405 and 1406 were marked by a civil war at the heart of the realm, and from that point on Majapahit's East Javanese home base was wracked by political dissension. By 1410 its power to the west of the island had disintegrated, and by 1428 it had lost control over the western part of Java.

The survival of the newly established port of Malacca was ensured by Chinese interests in the straits region. Between 1405 and 1431 the Ming court sent out seven fleets to what the Chinese called the Southern Ocean. On the first voyage, Admiral Zheng He, a Chinese Muslim originally from Yunnan Province, commanded an armada of sixty-two ships, with 27,000 people aboard (Fitzgerald, 1972: 88). After establishing contact with pepper merchants in northern Sumatra, he became concerned about security in the strait and so proceeded to destroy a nest of Chinese pirates that had grown up at Palembang. He then offered Malacca's ruler, Paramesvara, security in the form of a special relationship with China. If in 1405 the survival of Malacca was thus by no means guaranteed, the relationship it forged with Zheng He would protect it for decades, until the Chinese government abruptly abandoned its overseas expeditions in the 1430s. By that time, however, Malacca was securely rooted and was thereafter able to establish a commercial relationship with the ports on Java's north coast.

By the end of the fifteenth century Malacca had become the preeminent port of the maritime realm, with the result that traders no longer found it necessary to go to Majapahit for the fine spices. In the early sixteenth century one Portuguese adventurer enthusiastically counted merchants in Malacca's harbor hailing from some sixty different places, including Ethiopia and the East African ports of Kilwa and Malindi. At the same time, the Banda Islanders were producing some twelve hundred metric tons of nutmeg and one hundred metric tons of mace each year, while the islands off Halmahera's coast were delivering twelve hundred metric tons of cloves (Curtin, 1984: 130–32). In addition, the north Sumatran pepper ports were exporting thousands of tons of pepper annually (Simkin, 1968: 165).

## The Establishment of Muslim Mataram

By the middle of the fifteenth century Majapahit was no more than a troubled local power in eastern Java. The end did not come, however, until 1513, when a coalition of Muslim coastal communities on the island's north coast attacked the kingdom's very core. In 1528 they captured the Majapahit center, forcing the royal family to flee the island for refuge on Bali. As we have noted above, the victors established a new kingdom called Mataram, reviving the name of a tenth-century central Javanese kingdom, which had had its capital at Medang (Kulke, 1991: 17). Soon almost all who had lived within the realm of Majapahit had become Muslim. The principal exception remains the people of Bali, where the Hindu-Buddhist heritage of the islands continues to flourish.

The new Muslim Mataram placed its capital at Jogjakarta. Thus, after many centuries, a preeminent court reigned once more over the temple-covered rice plains of Central Java. Actually, during the period of East Java's hegemony, neither the economy nor the culture of Central Java had suffered a significant decline. Roads had been built from the rice plain to the northern ports. Archeological evidence attests to the presence of imported Chinese ceramics, an indicator of prosperity. In spite of its economic well-being, however, the new Mataram would never possess the power or the large realm that Majapahit had commanded. Like earlier Central Javanese kingdoms that had flourished in the centuries of the temple-boom, Mataram was essentially a local power; its influence did not extend beyond Java. Following Majapahit's demise, there were in fact many small powers in the maritime realm, many sultans, and all of them jealous of their local prerogatives. Nonetheless, the center at Jogjakarta prospered, and to this day it remains a lively cultural center, where the traditional arts and crafts still flourish.

# BIBLIOGRAPHY

Abu-Lughod, Janet L. 1989. *Before European Hegemony: The World System A.D. 1250–1350*. New York: Oxford University Press.

Bellwood, Peter. 1979. *Man's Conquest of the Pacific*. New York: Oxford University Press.

———. 1985. *Prehistory of the Indo-Malaysian Archipelago*. Orlando, Fla.: Academic Press.

———. 1992. "Southeast Asia before History," in Tarling, ed., 1992: 55–136.

Bellwood, Peter, and Matussin bin Omar. 1980. "Trade Patterns and Political Developments in Brunei and Adjacent Areas, A.D. 700–1500." *Brunei Museum Journal* 4 (4):155–79.

Bickmore, Albert S. 1869. *Travels in the East Indian Archipelago*. New York: D. Appleton and Company.

Bingham, Woodbridge, Hilary Conroy, and Frank W. Ikle. 1974. *A History of Asia,* Vol. 1. Boston: Allyn and Bacon.

Bray, Francesca. 1986. *The Rice Economies: Technology and Development in Asian Societies*. Berkeley: University of California Press.

Brierley, Joanna Hall. 1994. *Spices: The Story of Indonesia's Spice Trade*. Kuala Lumpur: Oxford University Press.

Bronson, Bennet, and Jan Wisseman. 1978. "Palembang as Srivijaya: The Lateness of Early Cities in Southern Southeast Asia." *Asian Perspectives* 19 (2): 220–39.

Chandra, Lokesh, Swarajya Prakash Gupta, Devendra Swarup, and Sitaram Goel, eds. 1970. *India's Contribution to World Thought and Culture*. Triplicane, India: Vivekananda Rock Memorial Committee.

Chandra, Moti. 1977. *Trade and Trade Routes in Ancient India*. New Delhi: Abhinav Publications.

Chau Ju-kua [Zhao Rugua]. *Gazeteer of Foreign Peoples and Products*. See Hirth and Rockhill, 1966.

Chaudhuri, K. N. 1985. *Trade and Civilization in the Indian Ocean: An Economic History from the Rise of Islam to 1750*. Cambridge: Cambridge University Press.

Chittick, H. Neville, and Robert I. Rotberg, eds. 1975. *East Africa and the Orient: Cultural Syntheses in Pre-Colonial Times*. New York and London: Africana Publishing Company (A Division of Holmes and Meier Publishers, Inc.).

Chou Ta-kuan [Zhou Daguan]. *Customs of Cambodia.* See d'Arcy Paul, 1987.

Christie, A. H. 1979. "Lin-i, Fu-nan, Java," in Smith and Watson, 1979: 281–87.

Coedès, George. 1971. *The Indianized States of Southeast Asia.* Ed. Walter E. Vella. Trans. Susan Brown Cowing. Honolulu: University Press of Hawaii.

Coomaraswamy, Ananda K. 1985. *History of Indian and Indonesian Art.* Leipzig: Karl W. Hiersemann, 1927. Repr. New York: Dover Publications.

Cowan, C. D., and O. W. Wolters, eds. 1976. *Southeast Asian History and Historiography.* Ithaca: Cornell University Press.

Crosby, Alfred W. 1972. *The Columbian Exchange: Biological and Cultural Consequences of 1492.* Westport, Conn.: Greenwood Press.

Curtin, Philip D. 1984. *Cross-Cultural Trade in World History.* New York: Cambridge University Press.

Dalton, Bill. 1991. *Indonesia Handbook,* 5th ed. Chico, Calif.: Moon Publishers.

d'Arcy Paul, J. Gilman, trans. 1987. *The Customs of Cambodia* by Zhou Daguan. Translated into English from the French version by Paul Pelliot of Zhou's original Chinese. Bangkok: The Siam Society.

Deshpande, M. N. 1970. "Campa—An Outpost of Indian Culture," in Chandra et al., eds., 1970: 475–82.

Diskul, M. C. Subhadradis, ed. 1980. *The Art of Srivijaya.* New York: Oxford University Press, with UNESCO.

Dumarcay, Jacques. 1978. *Borobudur.* Ed. and trans. Michael Smithies. Kuala Lumpur: Oxford University Press.

Fa Xian. 1956. *The Travels of Fa-hsien.* See Giles, 1956.

Fairbank, John K., ed. 1968. *The Chinese World Order.* Cambridge, Mass.: Harvard University Press.

Finney, Ben. 1994. "The Other Third of the Globe." *Journal of World History* 5 (2): 273–97.

Fischer, Otto. 1928. *Die Kunst Indiens, Chinas, und Japans.* Berlin: Propylaen-Verlay.

Fitzgerald, C. P. 1972. *The Southern Expansion of the Chinese.* New York: Praeger.

Fontein, Jan. 1971. "Ancient Indonesian Art," in Fontein, Soekmono, and Suleiman, 1971: 32–45.

———. 1990. *The Sculpture of Indonesia.* Washington, D.C.: National Gallery of Art, and New York: Harry N. Abrams, Inc.

Fontein, Jan, R. Soekmono, and Satyawati Suleiman. 1971. *Ancient Indonesian Art of the Central and Eastern Javanese Periods.* New York: Asia Society.

Francisco, Juan R. 1961. "Srivijaya and the Philippines: A Review." *Philippine Social Sciences and Humanities Review* 26 (1): 87–109.

———. 1971. *The Philippines and India: Essays in Ancient Cultural Relations.* Manila: National Book Store.

Geertz, Clifford. 1971. *Islam Observed: Religious Development in Morocco and Indonesia.* Chicago: University of Chicago Press.

———. 1980. *Negara: The Theatre State in Nineteenth-Century Bali.* Princeton: Princeton University Press.

Gesick, Lorraine, ed. 1983. *Centers, Symbols, and Hierarchies: Essays on the Classical States of Southeast Asia.* New Haven: Yale University Southeast Asia Studies, Monograph Series no. 26.

————. 1987. "The Invisible Entrepreneurs: The Structural Study of Women in Southeast Asia." Paper presented at the annual meeting of the American Historical Association, Washington, D.C., December.

Giles, F.H. 1956. *The Travels of Fa-hsien (399–414 A.D.) or Record of the Buddhistic Kingdoms.* Cambridge: Cambridge University Press, 1923. Repr. London: Routledge & Kegan Paul.

Gittinger, Mattiebelle. 1979. *Splendid Symbols: Textiles and Tradition in Indonesia.* Washington, D.C.: The Textile Museum.

————. 1982. *Master Dyers to the World: Technique and Trade in Early Indian Dyed Cotton Textiles.* Washington, D.C.: The Textile Museum.

Glover, Ian C. 1979. "The Late Prehistoric Period in Indonesia," in Smith and Watson, eds., 1979: 167–84.

Grottanelli, Vinigi. 1947. "Asiatic Influences on Somali Culture." *Ethnos* (Stockholm) 4: 153–81.

————. 1975. "The Peopling of the Horn of Africa," in Chittick and Rotberg, eds., 1975: 44–75.

Hall, Daniel G. E. 1968. *A History of Southeast Asia,* 3d ed. London: Macmillan, and New York: St. Martin's Press.

Hall, Kenneth. 1977. "The Coming of Islam to the Archipelago: A Reassessment," in Hutterer, ed., 1977: 213–31.

————. 1979. "The Expansion of Roman Trade in the Indian Ocean: An Indian Perspective." *The Elmira Review*: 36–42.

————. 1981a. "The Expansion of Maritime Trade in the Indian Ocean and Its Impact upon Early State Formation in the Malay World." *Review of Indonesian and Malaysian Affairs* 15 (2): 108–35.

————. 1981b. "Trade and Statecraft in the Western Archipelago at the Dawn of the European Age." *Journal of the Malaysian Branch of the Royal Asiatic Society* 54 (1): 21–47.

————. 1982. "The 'Indianization' of Funan: An Economic History of Southeast Asia's First State." *Journal of Southeast Asian Studies* 13 (1): 81–106.

————. 1985a. *Maritime Trade and State Development in Early Southeast Asia.* Honolulu: University of Hawaii Press.

————. 1985b. "Opening of the Malay World to European Trade in the Sixteenth Century." *Journal of the Malaysian Branch of the Royal Asiatic Society* 58 (2): 85–106.

————. 1988. "Maritime Trade and State Development in Fourteenth-Century Java," in H.I.H. Prince Takahito Mikasa, ed., *Cultural and Economic Relations between East and West: Sea Routes,* 97–110. Wiesbaden: Otto Harrassowitz.

————. 1989. "The Politics of Plunder in the Cham Realm of Early Vietnam," in Robert van Neil, ed., *Art and Politics in Southeast Asian History: Six Perspectives.* Honolulu: University of Hawaii, Center for Southeast Asia Studies, Southeast Asia Paper no. 32.

Hall, Kenneth, and John K. Whitmore, eds. 1976. *Explorations in Early Southeast Asian History: The Origins of Southeast Asian Statecraft.* Ann Arbor: University of Michigan, Center for South and Southeast Asian Studies. Michigan Papers on South and Southeast Asia no. 11.

Higham, Charles. 1989. *The Archaeology of Mainland Southeast Asia.* Cambridge and New York: Cambridge University Press.

Hill, A. H., trans. 1960. "Hikayat Raja-Raja Pasai." *Journal of the Malaysian Branch of the Royal Asiatic Society* 32 (2): 1–215.

Hirth, Friedrich, and W. W. Rockhill, trans. 1966. *Chau Ju-kua: His Work on the Chinese and Arab Trade in the Twelfth and Thirteenth Centuries, Entitled Chu-Fan-Chi.* [Zhu Fan Ji: *Gazeteer of Foreign Peoples and Products,* Quanzhou, China, 1225.] St. Petersburg: Imperial Academy of Science, 1911. Repr. Amsterdam: Oriental Press.

*Historical Relations across the Indian Ocean.* 1980. Report and Papers of the Meeting of Experts organized by UNESCO at Port Louis, Mauritius, from 15 to 19 July 1974. General History of Africa, Studies and Documents no. 3. Paris: UNESCO.

Holt, Claire. 1967. *Art in Indonesia: Continuities and Change.* Ithaca: Cornell University Press.

Honig, Pieter, and Frans Verdoorn, eds. 1945. *Science and Scientists in the Netherlands Indies.* New York: Board for the Netherlands Indies, Surinam, and Curaçao.

Hourani, George Fadlo. 1951. *Arab Seafaring in the Indian Ocean in Ancient and Early Medieval Times.* Princeton: Princeton University Press.

Hutterer, Karl L., ed. 1977. *Economic Exchange and Social Interaction in Southeast Asia: Perspectives from Prehistory, History, and Ethnography.* Ann Arbor: University of Michigan, Center for South and Southeast Asian Studies. Michigan Papers on South and Southeast Asia no. 13.

Ibrahim, Ahmad, Sharon Siddique, and Yasmin Hussain, eds. 1985. *Readings on Islam in Southeast Asia.* Singapore: Institute of Southeast Asian Studies.

Jacques, Claude. 1979. " 'Funan,' 'Chenla': The Reality Concealed by These Chinese Views of Indochina," in Smith and Watson, eds., 1979: 371–79.

Johns, Anthony H. 1966. "From Buddhism to Islam: An Interpretation of the Javanese Literature of the Transition." *Comparative Studies in Society and History* 9 (1): 40–50.

Johnstone, Paul. 1980. *The Seacraft of Prehistory.* Cambridge: Mass.: Harvard University Press.

Jones, A.M. 1971. *Africa and Indonesia: The Evidence of the Xylophone and Other Musical and Cultural Factors.* Leiden: E. J. Brill.

Kathirithamby-Wells, J., and John Villiers, eds. 1990. *The Southeast Asian Port and Polity: Rise and Demise.* Singapore: Singapore University Press.

Kobishanov, Y. M. 1981. "Aksom: Political System, Economics and Culture, First to Fourth Century," in Mokhtar, ed., 1981: 381–99.

Kulke, Hermann. 1986. "The Early and the Imperial Kingdom in Southeast Asian History," in Marr and Milner, eds., 1986: 1–22.

———. 1991. "Epigraphical References to the 'City' and the 'State' in Early Indonesia." *Indonesia* 52: 3–22.

Langdon, Robert. 1988. "Manioc, A Long Concealed Key to the Enigma of Easter Island." *Geographical Journal* 154 (3): 324–36.

Lansing, J. Stephen. 1983. *The Three Worlds of Bali.* New York: Praeger.

Lee, Yong Leng. 1982. *Southeast Asia: Essays in Political Geography.* Singapore: Singapore University Press.

Legge, John David. 1980. *Indonesia.* 3d ed. Sydney: Prentice-Hall of Australia.

Levtzion, Nehemia. 1979. *Conversion to Islam.* New York and London: Holmes and Meier Publishers.

Liu Xinru. 1985. "Early Commercial and Cultural Exchanges between India and China, First to Sixth Centuries A.D." Ph. D. dissertation, University of Pennsylvania.

———. 1988. *Ancient India and Ancient China: Trade and Religious Exchanges, A.D. 1–600.* Delhi: Oxford University Press.

———. 1995a. "Silks and Religions in Eurasia. c. A.D. 600–1200." *Journal of World History* 6 (1): 25–48.

———. 1995b. *The Silk Roads: Overland Trade and Cultural Interactions in Eurasia.* Forthcoming from Temple University Press, in the American Historical Association's Essay Series in Comparative and Global History.

Loofs-Wissowa, Helmut. 1986. "The True and the Corbel Arch in Mainland Southeast Asian Monumental Architecture," in Marr and Milner, eds., 1986: 239–53.

Ma Huan. *The Overall Survey of the Ocean's Shores.* See Mills, 1970.

McCloud, Donald G. 1986. *System and Process in Southeast Asia: The Evolution of a Region.* Boulder, Colo.: Westview Press.

McKinnon, E. Edwards. 1979. "A Note on the Discovery of Spur-Marked Yueh-type Sherds at Bukit Seguntang Palembang." *Journal of the Malaysian Branch of the Royal Asiatic Society* 52 (2): 41–48.

———. 1985. "Early Polities in Southern Sumatra: Some Preliminary Observations Based on Archaeological Evidence." *Indonesia* 40: 1–36.

McNeill, William H. 1963. *The Rise of the West: A History of the Human Community.* Chicago: University of Chicago Press.

———. 1976. *Plagues and Peoples.* Garden City, N.J.: Anchor Press/Doubleday.

Mango, Cyril A. 1980. *Byzantium: The Empire of New Rome.* New York: Charles Scribner's Sons.

———. 1984. *Byzantium and Its Image.* London: Variorum Reprints.

Manguin, Pierre-Yves. 1980. "The Southeast Asian Ship: An Historical Approach." *Journal of Southeast Asian Studies* 2 (2): 266–76.

———. 1986. "Ship-shape Societies: Boat Symbolism and Early Political Systems in the Malay World," in Marr and Milner, eds., 1986: 187–213.

———. 1987. "Etudes Sumatranaises. I. Palembang et Sriwijaya: Anciennes Hypothèses, Recherches Nouvelles." *Bulletin de l'Ecole française d'Extrême-Orient* 76: 337–402.

———. 1991. "The Merchant and the King: Political Myths of Southeast Asian Coastal Polities." *Indonesia* 52 (October): 41–54.

———. 1993. "Palembang and Sriwijaya: An Early Malay Harbour-City Rediscovered." *Journal of the Malaysian Branch of the Royal Asiatic Society* 66 (1): 23–46.

Marr, David G., and A. C. Milner, eds. 1986. *Southeast Asia in the 9th to the 14th Centuries.* Singapore: Institute of Southeast Asian Studies, Singapore, and the Research School of Pacific Studies, Australian National University.

Mau Vetter, Valerie. 1984. "In Search of Panji," in Morgan and Sears, eds., 1984: 31–50.

Meilink-Roelofsz, M.A.P. 1962. *Asian Trade and European Influence in the Indonesian Archipelago between 1500 and about 1630.* The Hague: Martinus Nijhoff.

Miksic, John N. 1990. *Borobudur: Golden Tales of the Buddhas.* Photographs by Marcello Tranchini. Boston: Shambhala.

Mills, J.V.G., trans. 1970. *Ma Huan Ying-yai Sheng-lan, The Overall Survey of the Ocean's Shores (1433).* Cambridge: Cambridge University Press for the Hakluyt Society.

Mokhtar, G., ed. 1981. *UNESCO General History of Africa.* Vol. 2: *Ancient Civilizations of Africa.* Berkeley: University of California Press.

Morgan, Stephanie, and Laurie Jo Sears, eds. 1984. *Aesthetic Tradition and Cultural Transition in Java and Bali.* Madison: University of Wisconsin, Center for Southeast Asian Studies.

Morton, W. Brown, III. 1983. "Indonesia Rescues Ancient Borobudur." *National Geographic* 163 (1): 126–42.

Muller, Kal. 1993. *Spice Islands: Exotic Eastern Indonesia.* Lincolnwood, Ill.: NTC Publishing Group.

Nilakanta Sastri, K. A. 1949. *History of Sri Vijaya.* Madras: University of Madras.

Peacock, B. A. V. 1979. "The Late Prehistory of the Malay Peninsula," in Smith and Watson, eds., 1979: 199–214.

Phillipson, D. W. 1981. "The Beginning of the Iron Age in Southern Africa," in Mokhtar, ed., 1981: 671–92.

Pigeaud, Theodore G. Th. 1960. *Java in the 14th Century, A Study in Cultural History: The Nagara-Kertagama by Rakaw Prapanca of Majapahit, 1365 A.E.* 3rd ed. 5 vols. The Hague: Martinus Nijhoff.

Piper, Jacqueline M. 1993. *Rice in South-East Asia: Cultures and Landscapes.* Kuala Lumpur: Oxford University Press.

Powers, Janet. 1993. "Indian Sea Voyages to the Islands of Gold." Paper presented at the Second International Conference of the World History Association, Honolulu, June.

Prapanca, *Nagara-Kertagama.* See Pigeaud, 1960.

Purseglove, J. W., E. G. Brown, C. L. Green, and S. R. J. Robbins. 1981. *Spices.* 2 vols. London: Longman.

Rawson, Philip. 1967. *The Art of Southeast Asia.* New York: Praeger.

Reid, Anthony. 1979. "Trade and the Problem of Royal Power in Aceh, Three Stages: c. 1550–1700," in Reid and Castles, eds., 1979: 45–55.

———. 1988. *Southeast Asia in the Age of Commerce, 1450–1680.* Vol. 1: *The Lands Below the Winds.* New Haven: Yale University Press.

Reid, Anthony, and Lance Castles, eds. 1979. *Pre-Colonial State Systems in Southeast Asia: The Malay Peninsula, Sumatra, Bali-Lombok, South Celebes.* Kuala Lumpur: Council of the Malaysian Branch of the Royal Asiatic Society, Monographs of the Malaysian Branch of the Royal Asiatic Society no. 6. First published in 1975.

Richards, J. F., ed. 1983. *Precious Metals in the Later Medieval and Early Modern Worlds.* Durham, N.C.: Carolina Academic Press.

Ridley, Henry N. 1912. *Spices.* London: Macmillan and Co.

Runciman, Steven. 1975. *Byzantine Style and Civilization.* Harmondsworth, Eng.: Penguin Books.

Sabloff, Jeremy A., and C. C. Lamberg-Karlovsky, eds. 1975. *Ancient Civilizations and Trade.* Albuquerque: University of New Mexico.

Schafer, Edward H. 1967. *The Vermilion Bird: Tang Images of the South.* Berkeley: University of California Press.

Scott, William Henry. 1984. *Prehispanic Materials for the Study of Philippine History.* Rev. ed. Quezon City: New Day.

Sears, Laurie Jo. 1984. "Epic Voyages: The Transmission of the *Ramayana* and *Mahabharata* from India to Java," in Morgan and Sears, eds., 1984: 1–30

Shahid, Irfan. 1984a. *Byzantium and the Arabs in the Fourth Century.* Washington, D.C.: Dumbarton Oaks.

———. 1984b. *Rome and the Arabs: A Prolegomenon to the Study of Byzantium and the Arabs.* Washington, D.C.: Dumbarton Oaks.

Simkin, C. G. F. 1968. *The Traditional Trade of Asia.* London: Oxford University Press.

Slametmuljana, B. Raden. 1976. *A Story of Majapahit.* Singapore: Singapore University Press.

Smith, R. B., and W. Watson, eds. 1979. *Early Southeast Asia.* New York and Kuala Lumpur: Oxford University Press.

Soekmono, R. 1971. "Notes on the Monuments of Ancient Indonesia," in Fontein, Soekmono, and Suleiman, 1971: 13–17.

———. 1976. *Chandi Borobudur: A Monument of Mankind.* Assen and Amsterdam: Van Gorcum, and Paris, The UNESCO Press.

Solheim, William G., II. 1965. "Indonesian Culture and Malagasy Origins." *Taloha* 1: 33–42.

———. 1975. "Reflections on the New Data of Southeast Asian Prehistory: Austronesian Origin and Consequence." *Asian Perspectives* 18 (2): 146–60.

Sopher, David E. 1977. *The Sea Nomads: A Study of the Maritime Boat People of Southeast Asia.* Singapore: National Museum Singapore. First published in 1965.

Southall, Aidan. 1975. "The Problem of Malagasy Origins," in Chittick and Rotberg, eds., 1975: 192–215.

Suleiman, Satyawati. 1980. "The History and Art of Srivijaya," in Diskul, ed., 1980: 1–20.

Sutaarga, Mohammed Amir. 1971. "Preface," in Fontein, Soekmono, and Suleiman, eds., 1971: 9–10.

Swearer, Donald K. 1981. *Buddhism and Society in Southeast Asia.* Chambersburg, Pa: Anima Books.

Takakusu, Junjiro, trans. 1896. *A Record of the Buddhist Religion as Practiced in India and the Malay Archipelago (A.D. 671–695) by I-Tsing.* Oxford: Clarendon Press.

Tarling, Nicholas, ed. 1992. *The Cambridge History of Southeast Asia.* Vol. 1: *From Early Times to c. 1800.* Cambridge and New York: Cambridge University Press.

Taylor, Keith. 1976. "Madagascar in the Ancient Malayo-Polynesian Myths," in Hall and Whitmore, eds., 1976.

———. 1992. "The Early Kingdoms," in Tarling, ed., 1992: 137–82.

Thapar, Romila. 1966. *A History of India,* Vol. 1. Harmondsworth, Eng.: Penguin Books.

Tibbetts, G. R. 1979. *A Study of the Arabic Texts Containing Material on South-East Asia.* Leiden: E. J. Brill.

Tirtaamidjaja, N. 1966. *Batik: Pola and Tjorak—Pattern and Motif.* English text by B. R. O. G. Anderson. Jakarta: Penerbit Djambatan.

van Leur, J. C. 1955. *Indonesian Trade and Society: Essays in Asian Social and Economic History.* The Hague and Bandung: W. van Hoeve, Ltd.

van Neil, Robert. 1989. *Art and Politics in Southeast Asian History.* Honolulu: University of Hawaii, Center for Southeast Asian Studies, Southeast Asia Paper no. 32.

van Setten van der Meer, N. C. 1979. *Sawah Cultivation in Ancient Java: Aspects of Development during the Indo-Javanese Period, 5th to 15th Century.* Canberra: Australian National University Press.

Verin, Pierre. 1975. "Austronesian Contributions to the Culture of Madagascar: Some Archaeological Problems," in Chittick and Rotberg, eds., 1975: 164–91.

————. 1981. "Madagascar," in Mokhtar, ed., 1981: 693–717.

Villiers, John. 1981. "Trade and Society in the Banda Islands in the Sixteenth Century." *Modern Asian Studies* 15 (4): 723–50.

Wagner, Frits A. 1959. *Indonesia: The Art of an Island Group.* Trans. Ann E. Keep. New York: McGraw-Hill.

Wang Gungwu. 1958. "The Nanhai Trade: A Study of the Early History of Chinese Trade in the South China Sea." *Journal of the Malaysian Branch of the Royal Asiatic Society* 31 (2): 1–135.

————. 1968. "Early Ming Relations with Southeast Asia: A Background Essay," in Fairbank, ed., 1968: 34–62.

Watson, Andrew M. 1983. *Agricultural Innovation in the Early Islamic World: The Diffusion of Crops and Farming Techniques, 700–1100.* Cambridge: Cambridge University Press.

Wheatley, Paul. 1959. "Sung Maritime Trade." *Journal of the Malayan Branch of the Royal Asiatic Society* 32 (2): 5–140.

————. 1964. *Impressions of the Malay Peninsula in Ancient Times.* Singapore: Eastern Universities Press.

————. 1973. *The Golden Khersonese: Studies in the Historical Geography of the Malay Peninsula before A.D. 1500.* Repr. Westport, Conn.: Greenwood Press. First published in 1961, Kuala Lumpur: University of Malaya Press.

————. 1975a. "Analecta Sino-Africana Recensa," in Chittick and Rotberg, eds., 1975: 76–114.

————. 1975b. "Notes on Chinese Texts Containing References to East Africa," in Chittick and Rotberg, eds., 1975: 284–90.

————. 1975c. "Satyánṛta in Suvarṇadvīpa: From Reciprocity to Redistribution in Ancient Southeast Asia," in Sabloff and Lamberg-Karlovsky, eds., 1975: 227–83.

————. 1983. *Nagara and Commandery: The Origins of Southeast Asian Urban Traditions.* University of Chicago, Department of Geography, Research Papers nos. 207 and 208.

Whitmore, John K. 1977. "The Opening of Southeast Asia: Trading Patterns through the Centuries," in Hutterer, ed. 1977: 139–53.

Williams, Lea E. 1976. *Southeast Asia: A History.* New York: Oxford University Press.

Wisseman, Jan. 1977. "Markets and Trade in Pre-Madjapahit Java," in Hutterer, ed., 1977: 197–212.

Wisseman-Christie, Jan. 1983. "Raja and Rama: The Classical State in Early Java," in Gesick, ed., 1983: 9–44.

———. 1986. "Negara, Mandala, and Despotic State: Images of Early Java," in Marr and Milner, eds., 1986: 65–93.

———. 1991. "States without Cities: Demographic Trends in Early Java." *Indonesia* 52: 23–40.

Wolters, O. W. 1967. *Early Indonesian Commerce: A Study of the Origins of Srivijaya*. Ithaca: Cornell University Press.

———. 1970. *The Fall of Srivijaya in Malay History*. Ithaca: Cornell University Press.

———. 1979. "Studying Srivijaya." *Journal of the Malaysian Branch of the Royal Asiatic Society* 52 (2): 1–32.

———. 1982. *History, Culture, and Region in Southeast Asian Perspectives*. Singapore: Institute of Southeast Asian Studies.

———. 1986. "Restudying Some Chinese Writings on Sriwijaya." *Indonesia* 42: 1–41.

Wyatt, David K. 1995. "Southeast Asia." In Mary Beth Norton and Pamela Gerardi, *The American Historical Association's Guide to Historical Literature*. 3d. ed., vol. 1, section 16: 476–97. New York and Oxford: Oxford University Press.

Yi Jing. N.d. *A Record of the Buddhist Religion as Practiced in India and the Malay Archipelago*. See Takakusu, 1896.

Yu Ying-shih. 1967. *Trade and Expansion in Han China: A Study of the Structure of Sino-Barbarian Economic Relations*. Berkeley: University of California.

Zhao Rugua. *Gazeteer of Foreign Peoples and Products*. See Hirth and Rockhill, 1966.

Zhou Daguan. *The Customs of Cambodia*. See d'Arcy Paul, 1987.

Zwalf, W. 1985. *Buddhism: Art and Faith*. London: British Museum.

# INDEX

# ABOUT THE AUTHOR

**Lynda Norene Shaffer,** Professor of History at Tufts University, teaches and writes about Chinese, Native American, and world history. After completing her undergraduate work at the University of Texas, Austin, she received a Ph.D. in history from Columbia University. A founding member of the World History Association, she has served three terms on its National Council. Her publications include *Mao and the Workers: The Hunan Labor Movement, 1920–23; Native Americans Before 1492: The Moundbuilding Centers of the Eastern Woodlands;* and "Southernization," *Journal of World History* 5, 1: 1–21.